PUBLISH YOUR FIRST MAGAZINE

A PRACTICAL GUIDE FOR WANNABE PUBLISHERS

SECOND EDITION

BY
LORRAINE PHILLIPS

360 Books, LLC
Atlanta, GA

For direct links to ALL the resources presented throughout this book, please visit:

WWW. PUBLISH YOURFIRST MAGAZINE. COM

Author: Lorraine Phillips
Cover and interior design: Lorraine Phillips
Website: publishyourfirstmagazine.com

ISBN-10: 0-9889535-4-4
ISBN-13: 978-0-9889535-4-3

LCCN: 2015905709
Library of Congress subject headings:
1. Magazine publishing.
2. Periodicals—Publishing—United States.

Published by:
360 Books, LLC
PO Box 105603, #22430
Atlanta, GA 30348-5603
www.3sixtybooks.com

First Printing
Printed in the United States of America

Acknowledgements

Thank you to all those who continue to keep me encouraged: Veronica Phillips-Holly, Lady Cherry Igbinedion, Henrietta Girard, Victoria Girard, Barbara Niles, Kimberly Perdue-Sims, Sylvia Copeland, and Sharon Sylvester (who I'd also like to thank for my awesome author pic).

Thank you also to the original *SisterPower Magazine* members: Candice Bovian, Karen Cotter, Aleidra Gonzales, and the late Jackie Cornelius. Because of you all, the dream continues.

Table of Contents

Chapter 2: Planning Your Magazine

Chapter 3: Creating Your Table of Contents

Chapter 4: Putting It All Together

Chapter 5: Magazine Branding and Design

Chapter 6: Your Marketing Materials

Chapter 7: Production and Your Graphic Designer

Chapter 8: Working With Printers

PART II - CREATING AN ONLINE PRESENCE

Chapter 9: Your Magazine's Website

Chapter 10: The Set Up

Chapter 11: Your Magazine's Blog

Chapter 12: Preparing Search Engine-Friendly Web Pages

Chapter 13: Being Web Savvy

Chapter 14: Social Media

PART III - TAKING CARE OF BUSINESS

Chapter 15: Monetizing Your Magazine

Chapter 16: Circulation and Distribution

Chapter 17: Keeping It Legal

Chapter 18: Your Business Plan

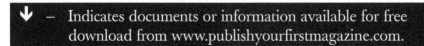

⬇ – Indicates documents or information available for free download from www.publishyourfirstmagazine.com.

Introduction

After a six-year run with *Publish Your First Magazine*, I knew it was time for a second edition. So much has changed, not only in the magazine publishing industry, but throughout the world in general. One of the biggest factors for that change is our level of connectivity to the internet, along with the explosive growth and use of smartphones and tablets, signifying that the way we consume media has forever been changed. Now almost anything you can possibly think of is literally a click away.

It's fair to say that the print magazine publishing industry has suffered somewhat in the process. The steady migration of audiences to digital has inevitably impacted the advertising sales business model that most magazines previously relied on. As an example, in late 2012 *Newsweek* magazine succumbed to the pressure, transitioned to all-digital, and folded its print edition. But what they found in the process was that there was still a high demand for print—readers urged them to go back into print in a voice that was so loud it couldn't be ignored (to which they later obliged in 2014). In seeking to satisfy reader demands, however, they realized that the business model they had previously operated under would no longer be feasible in today's environment and that it would be necessary to depend more heavily on subscribers, as opposed to advertisers, in order to pay the bills. And that's exactly where we find ourselves in the industry today.

Magazines (niche magazines in particular) are essentially becoming premium products—somewhat "couture" if you will—taking a lot of time to create, costing a significant amount to produce, being almost tailor-made to their audiences, manufactured to a high level of quality, containing little or no advertising, and consequently, expensive to buy. It just has to be that way in order for them to survive.

Due to this changing landscape, you might say that the days when a magazine could expect to survive as a print only product are over and that that particular business model (unless you're Condé Nast of course) could even be considered antiquated at this time. It is necessary for the publishers of today to get creative and figure out how their magazines can exist as a number of different entities and through a variety of mediums.

How will you leverage your website? Will you include a blog that's regularly updated with useful, engaging, relevant content? How do you plan to use social media to find and connect with your audience? Do you plan on creating an app or a tablet edition that will carry advertising? How about hosting events or giving lectures? Or even selling paraphernalia? In my recent book, *So I Published A Magazine: Conversations with Independent Publishers Around the Globe*, what I found is that although the print version of a magazine publisher's business was the core and bedrock of the brand (and yes, most were operating at profit), their publications actually existed over many mediums. I started out seeking to interview *magazine* publishers and ended up finding out that they are actually carrying out a million other interesting, money-generating activities as well.

Of course, the web would be considered the most important, and the Association of Magazine Media (MPA) has recognized that yesterday's print magazine company is today's magazine media company. Realizing the importance of a publisher being able to capture these new and imperative statistics, they took to task and devised a system that could. I quote: "Magazine Media 360° is a newly created industry metric that captures demand for magazine media content by measuring audiences across multiple platforms and formats (including print and digital editions, websites, video, and social media) to provide a comprehensive and accurate picture of magazine media vitality."

Thus far, these cross-platform far-reaching statistics have revealed that magazine audiences are growing at a steady rate, with audience increases being experienced by many different publishing companies and titles of varying audience sizes. This is great news for all magazine publishers and this information has now rendered the "print is dead" movement silent. It's not that print is dead at all, it's just that today a magazine has to exist in many different forms, and this book has been written with the contemporary perspective in mind. We'll not only cover various topics on print publishing, but also subjects like web setup, blogs, blogging, blog promotion, WordPress and its essential plug-ins, SEO, social media, social media listening tools—the whole gamut. Today's publishing toolset is very different from that of yesterday, and I hope you find this updated, expanded edition to be a great start on your journey into the very exciting world of magazine publishing. Here's wishing you every success in your publishing endeavors!

Lorraine Phillips

PART I

Creating
Your Magazine

Chapter 1:
The Framework

What is a Magazine?

"A magazine is not just a pound of paper. A magazine is a bunch of people with special interests and ideas communicating with a larger group who share the dedication to those interests."
–John Mack Carter

A magazine is really a hard thing to define when you think about it, as it means many different things to different people. I looked up the definition in Webster's dictionary, and it was so boring that I almost fell asleep reading it. Whatever it described in there (and I won't bore you with it here) was not the "thing" that I had previously worked on. It was exciting . . . with twists, turns, and challenges every day. It was the reason I got up every morning, especially after I quit my job way back when to pursue my dream full-time. I much prefer that definition by John Mack Carter; it's something I can identify with, so I think we'll stick with it.

The Three Types of Magazines

There are three types of magazines:

Consumer magazines: Consumer magazines are general or special interest magazines that are marketed to the public. The main purpose of these types of magazines is to entertain, sell products, and promote viewpoints. More often than not, they contain some form of advertising. Examples of consumer magazines include *Reader's Digest*, *i-D*, and *O, The Oprah Magazine*.

Trade magazines: Trade magazines are business-to-business magazines whose audience consists of readers in a particular trade or profession. Most will contain technical jargon that is not easily consumed by the general public. Although some trade magazines may be available on newsstands (e.g., *ComputerUser*, *Communication Arts*, etc.), most are sold through subscription only. Examples of trade magazines include *AJN: American Journal of Nursing* and *Cognitive Psychology*.

Other: Magazines that cannot be defined as being either consumer or trade fall into this category.

Organizational Structure

Although you may be a one-man or one-woman team, a print magazine will typically comprise the following departments. I have listed them in what I consider to be the order of importance. My reasoning is that the business department is responsible for planning, strategizing, and putting all the necessary parts together that should allow for a magazine to be profitable; and all other departments will follow and get direction from there.

Editorial, design, and production are responsible for creating a publication that will resonate with the target audience, who will in turn be made aware of the magazine's existence through effective marketing and promotions. Circulation is responsible for pulling in the numbers to attract advertisers or other entities. And lastly, the administration department provides support by performing general housekeeping duties.

Business: Responsible for the overall strategic vision and direction of the publication.

Editorial: Accountable for the magazine's content and tone.

Design: Visually creates the look and style of the magazine.

Production: Physically or technically produces the magazine on budget and to specification.

Promotion: Publicizes and advertises the magazine to advertisers; advertising agencies; potential readers; trade, professional, and business entities; interest groups; and other constituencies that are served by the magazine.

Circulation: Acquires, finds, and keeps readers through single-copy sales, subscriptions, free distribution, or other means.

Advertising: Handles, sells, and manages the magazine's advertising, which can often vital to its survival and success. This may be the only revenue source for trade and business magazines.

Administration: Keeps the books, pays the bills, invoices advertisers, processes payroll, completes forms, and generates reports.

Positions and Duties

CREATIVE

Editor in Chief/Editorial Director: Responsible for setting the vision, tone, style, look, and feel of the publication. Plans and directs the editorial process from concept through to publication. The official go-to person for any editorial issues. Duties may include writing articles, developing story ideas, approving layouts, as well as assisting with business strategic planning and development.

Executive Editor: Reports directly to the editorial director. Performs both managerial and editorial duties, keeping the magazine on schedule by enforcing strict deadlines. He or she also pitches in by preparing, assigning, and editing articles and doing whatever else is necessary to keep the magazine on track and on time.

Senior Editor: Writes, edits, proofreads, and copyedits articles. Helps assign articles to writers, making sure they understand the specific requirements. Other names for this title can include feature editor, beauty editor, fashion editor, and so forth.

Associate Editor: A staff editorial person who supports and assists the editor by writing, editing, and assigning material as required. May also be responsible for composing titles, subtitles, and captions.

Staff Writer: Resident staff member who writes and contributes articles to the magazine.

Contributing Editor: These writers are experts in the field that the magazine covers. This title may also be given to regular freelance writers with whom the magazine wishes to maintain a relationship.

Fact-Checker: Researches submitted articles, checking them for accuracy and correctness.

Copy Editor: Copy editors are not proofreaders. They check written material in its original form before layout and design, looking for and correcting errors in grammar, spelling, usage, and style. They also check articles for form, length, and completeness.

Proofreader: Checks over the final proof for typographical and mechanical errors.

Editorial Assistant: An entry-level position that supports more senior editors. Duties include researching information, setting up interviews, returning calls, making copies, and filing.

Website Editor: Responsible for creating and editing web content.

Creative Director/Art Director: Oversees the artistic design of the magazine and works closely with the editorial director to ensure the design is consistent with the editorial philosophy.

Graphic Designer: A graphic designer (also known as a graphic artist or communications designer) plans, analyzes, and creates visual solutions to communications problems. On a magazine, the graphic designer is responsible for physically creating exactly what the art director envisions, using color, type, illustration, photography, and various print and layout techniques to create a design that effectively communicates and appeals to its intended audience.

Photo Editor: Responsible for assigning visuals and images to magazine stories. Can also be tasked with maintaining, cataloging, and storing images.

DIGITAL

Programmer/Web Developer/Webmaster: Responsible or the creation and technical upkeep of a site. May specialize in programming languages such as HTML5, CSS, JavaScript, PHP, AJAX, and others.

WordPress Developer: Specializes in installing or creating WordPress themes, widgets, and plug-ins. May edit and customize existing themes or create one from scratch to specification. Typical skills for the position include HTML5, CSS, PHP, SQL, and JavaScript. (Depending on the content management system selected, this title could also be Drupal Developer, Joomla Developer, and so forth.)

Graphical User Interface Designer or User Experience Designer: Responsible for designing visuals (such as windows, icons, and menus) for an interface that provides users with the best possible experience and allows for simple, efficient, intuitive actions.

Animator: Adds interactive elements (such as quizzes and polls) to a publication through animations that are usually created using JavaScript or HTML5.

Videographer: Records, edits, and produces video projects using equipment and software.

Audio Engineer: Records, edits, and mixes audio sound using equipment and software.

Social Media Strategist: Maintains and fosters relationships online. Responsible for implementing strategies that increase brand awareness, generate incoming traffic, encourage reader loyalty, and boost subscription sales.

Data Analyst: Responsible for collecting and analyzing data on magazine website usage and performance or social media statistics. Prepares reports and makes recommendations as appropriate.

BUSINESS

Publisher: Ensures the magazine's editorial and commercial success. Primarily oversees the business side of the publication and is ultimately responsible for its profitability. Duties can include budgeting, strategic planning, and ad development.

Circulation Director: Manages all paid circulation and is responsible for maintaining and expanding readership.

Marketing Director/Promotions Director: Responsible for publicity and promotions. For a magazine to be successful, it must sell itself to both readers and advertisers.

Production Director: Responsible for creating, coordinating, and overseeing the production schedule to ensure the magazine is produced on time. Helps staff members format material so that all pages are complete and technically accurate. May also oversee the entire press run.

Advertising Director: Manages a staff of ad sales reps and is responsible for generating advertising in the magazine through direct selling and promotional activities.

Ad Sales Rep: Makes actual sales calls to and sets up appointments with existing and prospective advertisers. Responsible for maintaining current accounts and generating new business.

Business Manager: Supervises internal office management and business affairs to ensure that the magazine is on stable financial ground in order to achieve long-term success.

Departments, Columns, and Features

A magazine's editorial is divided into three sections:

Departments: These are the parts or sections of the magazine that the reader becomes familiar with and expects to see in every issue. They offer consistency and establish the tone and voice of a publication. A department may be written by a different contributor every month. They should be well planned and executed and grouped together under one common topic so that an individual department may have from one to several articles.

Columns: These articles are usually written by an expert or by a famous or respected individual. They provide credibility for the magazine and are written by the same person every issue.

Features: These are the longer pieces in the magazine, usually four to six pages (or more) in length. They are unique to every issue and most clearly exhibit the magazine's philosophy.

Reasons for Failure and Success

Concrete data on failure rates for print magazines is extremely hard to come by. A study performed approximately ten years ago by industry expert, Samir A. Husni estimated that 60 percent of new magazines fail within their first year. Mr. Husni also found that if a magazine managed to make it past the first year, they would actually increase their chances for survival later on down the line. Further statistics revealed that 80 percent of magazines failed by their fourth year, with 90 percent of them failing by their tenth.

More recent studies conducted by The College of Saint Rose librarian Steve Black indicated that 34 percent of newly launched magazines that fell into the "best new magazine" category failed within the first five years, with 13 percent of those failing within the first. These numbers continue to rise, and as with most industries, the magazine publishing business has been adversely affected by, and is still somewhat suffering from, the economic climate of recent years.

Although it seems that the numbers have drastically improved from those of ten years ago, the fact remains that the magazine business can still be a volatile one. Results are not conclusive. However, it is important to understand some of the factors that can contribute to a magazine's failure or success. Know that a publication won't fail or succeed due to any one of the following reasons, but an examination of a few should indicate what kind of "health" your magazine is in. Refer to these often and make sure you are scoring higher on the side of success than on the side of failure.

Reasons for failure:
- Insufficient planning and research
- Insufficient budget and funds to cover magazine costs
- No clearly defined audience or target market
- Unfocused mission and editorial philosophy
- Inability to connect with readers
- The subject matter addresses a short-lived trend or fad that does not have an ongoing need for information
- Lack of effective marketing
- Inability to devise, or partner up, in order to create a significant distribution system that increases a magazine's visibility
- Unable to generate advertising income due to low circulation or poor visibility (without significant distribution)
- Bad design
- Unattractive covers and bylines that do not pull readers in
- Lackluster content
- Poor editorial direction
- Insufficient demand from consumers for the new publication
- Inexperienced management and staff

Reasons for success:
- Significant planning and research
- Sufficient funds to cover magazine costs until profits are expected
- A clearly defined audience and target market
- A highly focused mission and editorial philosophy
- A thorough understanding of audience wants and needs
- The magazine serves an ongoing need for information
- An effective marketing plan
- A distribution system or network that allows for high visibility
- Ability to attract advertisers and generate advertising income
- A great design that appeals to the intended audience
- Attractive covers and bylines that "force" readers to pick up and purchase—or subscribe to—the magazine
- Content that appeals to readers
- Great editorial direction
- High consumer demand
- Experienced management, staff, advisers, and freelancers

Chapter 2:
Planning Your Magazine

Is it Really a Magazine?

Before you begin this journey, it is important to answer the question of whether this is truly a magazine. While the subject matter may be of interest to you, how can determine that others will find it interesting also? How do you know that these particular information needs are not already being met elsewhere . . . online or otherwise? What will you do that is different? What unique perspective will you offer? And most importantly, how do you plan to engage your audience so that they might become loyal readers and subscribers?

Who are your readers? Do you have them defined? Is it a special niche audience? And if so, how do you plan to find them and make them aware of your new publication? How familiar are you with the market? What are their interests, problems, frustrations, concerns, dreams, aspirations, and fears? Are you an authority on the subject, or can you locate those who are? Is this a fad, or will readers have continuing information needs? Can you evolve editorially with each issue, or do you have enough information and ideas for just a few? Ultimately, is this really something people want to read about, will continue reading about, and why?

Study the Competition

To help answer some of the questions above, it is imperative that you study your competition. Check other magazines and popular magazine blogs that are somewhat similar in content. Media kits will also provide you a lot of relevant "insider" information.

Look at how the magazines are formatted and designed. Can you compete? Who currently advertises with them? What are their most popular topics? Check their social network accounts and see the number of followers there. How often do they update their pages? Check the level of engagement, which will really give you an idea of how the subject matter is being received. While doing your research, pay special attention to the types of questions people ask or the requests they make to see if you notice any recurring patterns. This can provide clues as to what types of editorial opportunities exist and what content you may need to focus on providing.

Next, hit Amazon.com and look at the customer reviews of competing or similar magazines. You can unearth a gold mine of information as you look at the comments to determine what a magazine is doing well and how it is satisfying its readers. Low-rated comments will also provide clues as to what you need to improve on to capture the attention of your desired audience. Build a long list of what your competitors do well (the pros) and not so well (the cons). This list can help you understand exactly what you need to do with your publication in the marketplace. Do not underestimate the tremendous amount of insight that can be gained from carrying out an exercise such as this.

All in all, do your homework and don't ignore the signs. You are about to invest a great deal of time and money into your project, so you need to know for sure that what "it" is is actually a magazine that there's a real audience for. Visit trade shows and conferences. Talk to peers, experts in the field, and special interest groups. Go to social networks or topic-specific chat rooms and post polls or surveys. Do everything you need to do to get significant feedback on your idea before you proceed.

Your Editorial Philosophy

Everything starts with a vision. If you don't know where you're going, you'll end up somewhere else.

Now that you have taken the time to study the competition, it's time to create your editorial philosophy, which will act as the guiding light for your new publication. When making various decisions concerning your magazine (even something as simple as deciding on the appropriateness of an article), you can always refer back to your philosophy and see whether it satisfies the criteria presented there.

To create an effective mission, you really have to understand what your audience expects from your magazine. What will you do to satisfy those needs? Understand the function of your magazine in the life of your reader after all, you'll be creating the publication for them. Your editorial philosophy should answer questions like:

- What is the magazine's main focus?
- What is its concept and purpose?
- What should it accomplish or achieve?
- Who is it aimed at?
- How am I different from other publications in the marketplace?

- Why is there a need for its existence?
- What are the main areas of interest?
- What is the personality (voice or tone) of the publication?

EXAMPLE EDITORIAL PHILOSOPHY FOR SISTERPOWER MAGAZINE

SisterPower Magazine is an inspirational magazine that instigates a woman's spiritual journey to inner strength, inner beauty, and inner peace. The main focus includes affirmations, spirituality, self-improvement, and empowerment. The message will be delivered in a friendly, conversational tone, where readers will be able to say, "That is exactly what I was thinking and feeling, and that's the way I would have expressed it myself." This platform has been created for women to share their thoughts, feelings, and life experiences, providing them with a voice and a place where they can be heard, validated, and ultimately understood.

Your Editorial Formula

In determining your magazine's editorial formula, you will need to answer the following questions:

- What is the frequency of publication? (Monthly, quarterly, etc.)
- How much will I charge per issue?
- What will be the price for subscriptions?

- How many pages will there be?
- How many of these pages will be dedicated for editorial?
- Will there be any ads?
- If so, how many of those pages will be dedicated to advertising? (See note below)
- What is the CPM? (See the following page for explanation)
- How many departments will there be?
- How many columns?
- How many features?
- What will be the average length of a feature?
- Will there be any special content? (Pullouts, etc.)

To answer these questions, it's a good idea to create a grid similar to that found overleaf in Figure 1 and write down the editorial formula for magazines that are somewhat similar to yours. Although you may not be able to accurately fill in all the information at this time, you can "guesstimate" the figures based upon your research and update as you gain more knowledge as you complete upcoming chapters.

Most start-up magazines contain little or no advertising. You'll want to keep this in mind as you build your plan to make your magazine profitable. Printing will be your greatest expense, so the more pages you print, the more expensive it will be (although there are ways to cut your printing costs, as we will discuss in Chapter 8). To be eligible for newsstand distribution, your magazine should be sixty-four pages or more in length and published at least four times a year.

See "Monetizing Your Magazine" in Chapter 15, to understand how to figure out your costs and how to compute the amount of advertising (if you have decided to build advertising in as a part of your revenue model) that will need to be sold in each issue to make your magazine profitable.

Note: According to the most recent study on the advertising-to-editorial ratio in US magazines by The Statistics Portal (www.statista.com), print magazines carried 53.7 percent editorial vs. 46.3 percent advertising pages.

CPM: Print magazines measure ad rates according to CPM (cost per thousand), which indicates the cost for an advertiser to reach 1,000 readers. It is calculated by dividing the page price by circulation. For instance, if your circulation is 5,000 and you charge $1,000 for a full-page ad, then your CPM = $1,000 / 5 = $200, meaning that it will cost an advertiser $200 to reach 1,000 readers. This term is also used for online marketing where CPM is the cost per 1,000 impressions. For example, a CPM of $1 would indicate a cost of $1 per 1,000 ad views.

Figure 1: Editorial Formula Grid

	Magazine A	Magazine B	Magazine C	Your Magazine
Issue studied?	March 2017	Jan 2017	June 2017	N/A
Frequency?	Monthly	Bi-monthly	Quarterly	?
Price?	$4.95	$9.00	$18.00	?
Subscription price?	$50.00	$40.00	$60.00	?
Total no. of pages?	198	296	176	?
No. of advertising pages (%)?	70 (47%)	60 (47%)	47 (27%)	?
No. of editorial pages (%)?	78 (53%)	68 (53%)	128 (73%)	?
Advertising-to-editorial ratio?	7:8	7:8	1:3	?
CPM?	50	31	N/A	?
No. of editorial sections?	7	9	7	?
No. of departments?	10	17	21	?
No. of columns?	1	2	2	?
No. of features?	6	8	5	?
Average feature length?	6 pages	7 pages	4 pages	?
Special content included?	None	Bookmark	Calendar pullout	?

Naming Your Magazine

Now that both your editorial philosophy and formula is in place and you're beginning to understand the direction of your magazine, it's time to give it a name. A magazine's name is one of its most important attributes, as it conveys the entire message to your readers. It's the first thing someone will see or hear whether it's in conversation, as a search engine result, on the cover, or as the logo on your website. It's also a very important marketing tool that has to quickly and accurately communicate the correct message to your audience.

Think of the qualities that you want your magazine to project and be identified with. Is the name descriptive? Is it easy to spell? Can readers pronounce it with ease? Is it memorable, or is it something that can easily be forgotten? And lastly, can it be visually made into a great logo and website header?

Another consideration in name choice will be whether the domain name is available. You can check this at Go Daddy (www.godaddy.com). You should also check Facebook, Instagram, and other social networks to determine whether the name is available across those platforms as well. To have consistency on all (which I highly recommend) you may have to opt for some type of variation of your originally thought-out name, or if you'd definitely like to keep the originally thought of name, then you may need to create a slight variation that you use across the social networks.

After you have narrowed your name choices down to a few, try them out on family and friends. Ask them what the name means to them and what image it conjures up. Find out if they can easily understand, pronounce, and spell it.

Next, verify that you are not infringing on any copyrights or trademarks and that no one else is using the name by performing searches at both the US Copyright Office (www.copyright.gov) and the US Patent and Trademark Office (www.uspto.gov). You should also check with your local county clerk's office to see whether the name is already on the list of fictitious or assumed business names in your county. Once you've completed all these steps and finalized your name choice, then I recommend that you go ahead and register it right away.

> **Note:** For more information on choosing and registering a domain, please see my top ten rules for selecting a domain name in Chapter 10 (page 118) under "Choosing Your Host and Registering Your Domain."

Your Magazine's Bar Code

A bar code, also known as a Universal Product Code (UPC), is a unique fourteen-digit number that allows retailers to track the sales of magazines through computerized inventory control systems. Most distributors require UPC bar codes, and you will need one if aiming for distribution with some of the larger chain bookstores.

The UPC is made up of five parts: the Beginning Check Digit, the Manufacturer's Code, the BIPAD, the End Check Digit, and the Issue Code (also known as the UPC Add-On Code).

Figure 2: Example Bar Code

The beginning check digit: Indicates the type of product being scanned. For a magazine this will usually be 0 or 7.

The manufacturer's code: The manufacturer's ID.

The BIPAD: The five-digit BIPAD number never changes. It is the permanent identification of a magazine's title for the life of the magazine (see below).

The end check digit: A check digit calculated by a formula from the UPC's first eleven digits; used to ensure that the code has been scanned correctly.

The issue code: This number changes with each issue. The issue code must be unique during a given year but can be repeated in subsequent years.

The current charge for a BIPAD number is $350. After paying the initial one-time setup fee, your UPC will cost $35 for each subsequent issue. For details and application forms, go to www.bipad.com.

BIPAD Inc. assigns you the actual BIPAD number, but you will have to contact PIPS, Inc. (Product Identification and Processing Systems) to have the electronic, machine-readable version of the bar code that actually goes on the cover generated. The charge for a single bar code is $35 and the website address is www.pips.com.

PIPS will need the following information:
• Name of magazine
• US cover price
• Canadian cover price
• BIPAD
• Full UPC
• Frequency (monthly, quarterly, etc.)
• Add-on or issue code
• EPS file format (Mac or PC)

- Delivery method (CD-ROM or email)
- Shipping address (for CD-ROM orders)
- Billing information

Note: If planning on working with a distributor you may want to hold off on purchasing your bar code, as this was later supplied to me for free by my distribution company.

Acquiring an ISSN

If you plan on working with or selling subscriptions to libraries, then you will need an International Standard Serial Number (ISSN). An ISSN is a unique eight-digit number that is assigned to a serial publication to identify the title, regardless of language or country where it is published. There is no charge for the use and assignment of an ISSN in the United States. For more information and ISSN application forms, visit www.loc.gov/issn.

Chapter 3:
Creating Your Table of Contents

Your Table of Contents

You've studied the competition and figured out exactly where you fit in in the marketplace, so now it's time to get brave and demonstrate how you plan to do that editorially. This is where you decide what your audience would like to read and select the topics you will cover editorially.

Using the structure provided in Chapter 1, think of your content in terms of departments (subjects that are grouped together under one common topic), columns (sections or articles that are usually written by an expert or a respected individual), and features (unique content that is neither a department nor a column but most clearly exhibits the magazine's philosophy).

Doing it this way will allow you to clearly arrange and organize your content offerings. Your table of contents will be vital in providing an overview of your magazine at one glance, so make sure to come up with clear, catchy, and descriptive titles that have the ability to draw readers in.

If you already have a website or a social media presence then you can simply visit those properties (and competitor sites too) and take note of what the hot, trending, or most popular topics are. After a while you may begin to notice subject patterns emerging. If they're actively talking about it online, then it's probably safe to assume that it's a topic readers will want to read or learn more about. Post questions or comments and brainstorm online. These are the folks who are going to buy your publication, so you might as well get them involved from the start by asking them what they'd like to read or learn more about.

Remember to look at competitor magazines also. You should have already compiled a list of their pros and cons which can also help to generate story ideas. Look at their actual articles: What can you do different? Is there a way to revise or update a story? How about expounding on an idea already presented? Or totally disagreeing with another?

After you have completed your investigative research and decided what subjects your audience will find interesting and useful, then you are ready to set up your departments and columns. Create your initial table of contents by starting with a description, deciding on a title, and then defining whether it will be either a department or a column. Features are the easy part, as they change with each issue and you just get creative with them every time. For me previously, as an editorial director, when a subject I wanted to discuss in the magazine didn't really fit into a department or column but went along with the titled theme of a particular issue, it usually wound up being a feature. Not brain science I know—but it worked.

To help you with brainstorming ideas for your table of contents, here are some examples of things that people want:

- To be liked and appreciated
- To find love and commitment
- To build a strong self-image
- To achieve better health and longer lives
- To lead more fulfilling lives
- To be more attractive to the opposite sex

Figure 3: Example Table of Contents for *SisterPower Magazine*

Title	Description	Article Type
My 2 Cents	Letter from the editor	Department
Table of Contents	Table of contents	Department
Holla!	Reader views and comments	Department
Contributor Credits	Contributing editors	Department
Wind Down Zone	Magazine final word offering food for thought until the next issue	Department
Shero	Ordinary women doing extraordinary things	Department
About Us	Focusing on sisters and sisterhood	Column
Chic Geek	High-tech gadget page	Column
CashFlow	Personal finance	Column
Her PRO-file	Entrepreneur spotlight (Female)	Department
His PRO-file	Entrepreneur spotlight (Male)	Department
Sister Sound Off	Commentary	Department
The Queens of Conversation	Live commentary with six participants that discuss various topics of interest	Department
Take It To The Streets	Reader Q and A section	Department
In His Eyes	Commentary from the male's perspective	Column
Ask The Harpers	Relationship advice from a husband and wife team	Department
SisterPower	Comic strip superhero	Department
Scopes	Horoscopes	Column
Creating The Balance	Creating utopia within	Column
HeadQuarters	Hair and beauty	Column
Work It!	Picture-intensive fitness instructional guide	Column
Fashion Forward	Highlighting the latest styles and fashions from around the world	Department
Your Health	Women's health issues	Column
Soulfood	Affirmations (x4)	N/A
Sister Sharon Shares	Relating the bible to life today	Column
Relations	Focusing on love, sex, and relationships	Column
Boarding Pass	Travel page	Department
Secret Confessions	Reader confessions	Department
For Fun: Crossword	Crossword	Department
For Fun: Quiz	Quiz	Department
For Fun: Carol's Corner	Carol's comedy corner (commentary)	Department
SisterPoems	Reader poetry submissions	Department

- To attain financial security and wealth
- To be entertained and have fun
- To find solutions to their problems
- To know how to save time and be more efficient
- To gain knowledge or expertise on a particular subject
- To learn how to perform a task
- To receive buying advice on products and services
- To be self-sufficient, including owning their own business
- To understand their place in the overall scheme of things
- To gain clarity and direction
- To be motivated and inspired
- To find inner peace
- To be successful
- To express themselves by sharing personal stories and experiences

Ultimately, your readers are looking for ways to enhance their lives in some way, shape, or form. Make sure to address these types of needs in your content offerings.

Where To Find Content

All publishers ask this question. Here are a few possible resources:

Yourself: You must strong opinions about—or an affiliation with—a subject matter otherwise you would have never come up with the idea of creating a magazine in the first place.

Your staff members or the people they know: Don't take this for granted. There's family, friends, and associates. Everyone knows an expert or someone with a great story to tell.

Your website: Post your writer's guidelines (see page 49) on your website for interested contributors.

Social media networks: Find experts, professionals, and writers specific to your particular genre by performing keyword searches on profiles or by joining groups that have a similar interest and connecting with the individuals that you find there.

Search engines: Pop a few terms that describe your particular subject matter into your favorite search engine and see what experts, websites, or topic-specific blogs come up in the results.

Specialized websites: Connect with journalists, bloggers, and other communications professionals and experts at websites such as Help A Reporter Out (www.helpareporter.com), and ProfNet from PR Newswire (www.prnewswire.com/profnet).

Freelance resources: To hire freelance writers, journalists, and bloggers, post requirements to sites such as Elance (www.elance.com), Freelancer (www.freelancer.com), and Guru (www.guru.com).

Reprints: These are previously published articles (either online, in print, or otherwise) that can be purchased for use within your own publication.

Free content available online: Some sites allow you to publish the articles found on their websites as long as you follow the guidelines as set out in the "terms of agreement." If you would rather not reprint the articles found there, then this is also a good way for you to find experts and specialists in your field. Such websites include Articlesbase (www.articlesbase.com), Articles Factory (www.articlesfactory.com), and EzineArticles (www.ezinearticles.com).

Organizations, associations, and special interest groups in your field: Find them online or offline in your area. Join social networking sites, chat rooms, discussion groups, newsgroups, and email lists to tell people all about your new publication and to publicize that you are looking for writers.

Universities and colleges: Find professors who are willing to share knowledge in their field of expertise.

Local journalism schools: Talk to educators, ask to use their most gifted students, and make arrangements for them to receive extra credit for their contributions.

Local writing clubs: Here you will find an abundance of eager writers who will be honored to contribute to your magazine.

Writing contests: This is a creative way of sourcing material.

Other newspapers and magazines (both online and offline): Scan these sources for story ideas or updates to previously published articles. Look for freelance writers who may post contact information along with their articles.

Classifieds: Advertise for writers either online (e.g., Craigslist) or offline (e.g., newspapers, writer's magazines, etc.).

WEBSITES FOR CONTENT IDEAS

Alltop (www.alltop.com)
Alltop collects the headlines of the latest stories from the best websites and blogs that cover a specific topic. It then groups these collections, or aggregations, into individual web pages and displays the five most recent headlines from these information sources. Topics run from adoption to zoology, with stories about photography, food, science, religion, celebrities, and hundreds of other subjects in between.

BuzzFeed (www.buzzfeed.com)
BuzzFeed claims to track the web's obsessions in real time.

Digg (www.digg.com)
Information curation service that provides the most relevant and compelling content to millions of users a month cutting through the clutter of the internet and making sense of all the noise in a way that you don't have to.

Engadget (www.engadget.com)
Engadget is a web magazine with daily coverage of everything new in gadgets and consumer electronics.

Google Alerts (www.google.com/alerts)
These are weekly, daily, or instantaneous alerts, sent to you via email, that contain the latest, most relevant Google results based on the keywords you select. Basically, the Google Alerts service allows you to create an automatic news finder.

Google News (news.google.com)
Google News is a computer-generated news site that aggregates headlines from more than 4,500 English-language news sources worldwide. Similar stories are then grouped together and displayed according to personalized interests.

Google Trends (www.google.com/trends/hottrends)
Google trends offers up-to-the-minute information on the hottest searches. It also allows you to compare the volume of searches between two or more terms.

How Stuff Works (www.howstuffworks.com)
Award-winning source of unbiased, easy-to-understand answers and explanations of how "things" in the world actually work.

Huffington Post (www.huffingtonpost.com)
Ranked as #1 on the 15 Most Popular Political Sites list by eBizMBA

Rank. The site offers news, blogs, and original content that cover politics, business, entertainment, environment, technology, popular media, lifestyle, culture, comedy, healthy living, women's interests, and local news.

lifehacker (www.lifehacker.com)
The number one productivity blog on the internet.

Mashable (www.mashable.com)
Leading source for news, information, and resources for the connected generation. Mashable reports on the importance of digital innovation and how it empowers and inspires people around the world.

popurls (www.popurls.com)
Known as the dashboard for the latest web buzz, it's a single page that encapsulates up-to-the-minute headlines from the most popular sites on the internet.

reddit (www.reddit.com)
Online community where users vote on which stories and discussions are important so the hottest stories rise to the top, while cooler stories sink to the bottom. It's the place you go to discover stories and conversations that you may never have heard of otherwise.

Social Media Examiner (www.stumbleupon.com)
Touted as a guide to the social media jungle this site helps businesses discover how to best use social media, blogs, and podcasts to connect with customers, drive traffic, generate awareness, and increase sales.

StumbleUpon (www.stumbleupon.com)
A social network that helps you discover and share unique, interesting websites by delivering high-quality pages that are matched to your personal preferences.

TechCrunch (www.techcrunch.com)
This media blog profiles start-ups, reviews new internet products, and reports on breaking tech news.

Techmeme (www.techmeme.com)
This single, easy-to-scan page tracks what's changing in technology in order to understand the cultural currents and business events that are reshaping our world.

Trendwatching.com (www.trendwatching.com)
This site features emerging consumer trends, insights, and related hands-on business ideas from around the world.

The Webby Awards (www.webbyawards.com)
The leading international award that honors excellence on the internet (also dubbed "The Oscars of the Internet"). Awards are presented across various categories such as: website, mobile, social, advertising, and online film and video.

99U (www.99u.com)
Daily insights on how to make ideas happen through in-depth interviews, articles, videos, and bite-size blog posts.

Creating Your Writers' Guidelines

All magazines will have different requirements based on their particular subject matter, audience, style, and tone. Your writers' guidelines describe exactly what you are looking for in articles to be considered for publication. A great resource can be found at Freelance Writing (www.freelancewriting. com), where you will find links to 882 magazine writers' guidelines across various subject categories. At a minimum your guidelines should contain:

An introduction to your magazine

EXAMPLE: Thank you for your interest in writing for *SisterPower Magazine*. *SisterPower* covers all aspects of a woman's life, featuring personal, first-person stories. Dubbed as a manual for women who want to make better choices, *SisterPower* aims to feed the soul, encourage, motivate, and inspire.

Description of the editorial style, voice, and tone of the magazine

EXAMPLE: The editorial voice of submitted works should be friendly, intimate, relaxed, and conversational. Very down-to-earth, just as if you were sitting around chatting with a bunch of friends. Where appropriate, please feel free to put as much of your personality, personal values, and thoughts into the article as possible. This is your article, from your point of view, so give people a taste of who you are, how you are feeling, and what you think.

Article length and expectations

EXAMPLE: Although we do not like to give a required length (as we feel that the content of a particular article should dictate its length), we would suggest that submissions not be longer than 2,000 words. In addition, to ensure review of your materials, please make sure you submit final drafts of your work. We have limited editorial staff and cannot spend time editing.

Directions on exactly how articles should be submitted

EXAMPLE: Submit articles and story pitches (an idea for an article) via email to *articles@SisterPower.com*. Put the words "EDITORIAL SUBMISSIONS" in the subject line and indicate the article category. We accept MS Word, PDF, TXT, and HTML files, as well as JPEG, TIFF, PSD, and AI picture files. If your work is in a format other than the aforementioned, please send the text of your query or submission in plain text in the body of your email to ensure that we can read the format of your file.

Information authors should provide

EXAMPLE: Please include your name, address, email address, and daytime and mobile numbers. If this is your first time submitting to us, please tell us about yourself, your experience, background as a writer, and your qualifications for writing a particular story. If you have any clips, please include a representative sampling (no more than three articles please).

What to expect after submitting a story

EXAMPLE: We do our best to respond to all inquiries, but be aware that we are sometimes inundated. If your writing sample(s) meets our requirements, then a member of staff will contact you. Allow at least two months for a response. If you have not heard back from us within this period, please assume that we will not be able to use your idea or submission at this time.

The topics you are interested in receiving

EXAMPLE: *SisterPower* is interested in receiving submissions on a variety of topics, including (but not limited to) the following:

- Emotional, spiritual, or physical well-being
- Motivational and inspirational pieces
- Personal experiences, true stories, and confessions
- Love, sex, and relationships
- Political or social issues
- Entertainment news
- Book, music, film, or video reviews
- Events coverage
- Hair and beauty
- Fashion
- Health and fitness

- Opinion pieces
- "How to" type stories (e.g., how to start your own business, how to fix your credit, etc.)
- Family
- Business advice
- Money and finance
- Home décor and gardening tips
- Food and recipes
- Travel
- Subjects from the male perspective
- Humor

Compensation offered

EXAMPLE: Pay rate is discussed on an individual basis and determined by the type of article submitted as well as the relevant experience of a writer.

Working with Graphics and Images

UNDERSTANDING RESOLUTION

Resolution refers to how sharp an image is. Images are often described as being either high-resolution (hi-res) or low-resolution (low-res) files. For print purposes, high-resolution files with a minimum value of 300 dpi should be used. Low-resolution graphics do not contain as much detail or information as high-resolution graphics and are only intended for screen display purposes. For instance, web graphics are usually 72 dpi, and although they may look good on-screen, they are not suitable for professional printing. To check an image's resolution in Photoshop, go to Image > Image Size.

VECTOR AND RASTER IMAGES

There are two types of computer graphics—vector graphics and raster graphics. Vector graphics are primarily used for professional printing. These images can be enlarged or reduced without any loss of quality, so it does not matter whether you put your logo on a business card or a full-sized poster; the image will appear with the same amount of detail. Vector images are created by using mathematical formulas, and enlarging or reducing an image simply results in a calculation being performed to produce that image. Examples of vector formats include AI (Adobe Illustrator), EPS (encapsulated postscript), and CDR (CorelDraw).

Raster, or bitmap images, are created using a grid of individual pixels that are each assigned a different color or shade. Scaling a bitmap file down will not result in loss of quality, but enlarging it will. The image loses detail and appears jagged around the edges. Examples of raster formats include BMP, TIFF, GIF, and JPEG files. For print purposes, only high-resolution TIFF and JPEG files should be utilized.

RGB AND CMYK

TV and computer monitors produce images using the RGB color model. This color mode is based on the theory that all visible colors can be created using the primary additive colors of red, green, and blue. When these colors are combined equally, they produce white, and when combined in different amounts, they produce a broad array of colors.

The printing world, on the other hand, operates in subtractive color mode, known as CMYK. CMYK refers to the four ink colors used by the printing press—cyan (blue), magenta (red), yellow, and black. In theory, cyan, magenta, and yellow (CMY) can print all colors, but the inks are not pure and produce murky colors so black is added to ensure quality printing.

An image that is in RGB mode is optimized for display on a computer monitor and must be converted to CMYK in order for your printer to be able to produce that image on paper. Not all colors you create in RGB mode can be reproduced in CMYK, so the conversion process may result in a slight color shift that may cause your image to appear a little different than expected once printed. To change or check the color mode of a graphic in Photoshop, go to Image > Mode.

SUMMING IT ALL UP

When preparing graphics for print, files should meet the following requirements:

- have a resolution of 300 dpi or higher
- either be in vector or raster (TIFF, JPEG or PDF) file formats, and
- appear in the CMYK color mode.

Using Stock Photography

To ensure you do not risk infringing on any existing copyrights, when not using original artwork it is best to acquire images from stock photography sites like those presented in the next section. Images found there will be licensed for specific purposes, so make sure you understand and follow the respective guidelines as presented on each site.

In general, there are two types of stock photography licenses available: royalty-free (RF) and rights-managed (RM). With a royalty-free license, you pay a flat fee that allows for unlimited use of a photo or illustration in any media as defined in the licensing agreement. On the other hand, a rights-managed photo is licensed for a one-time, specific use only. Fees are determined by the usage purpose which is defined according to numerous variables, including how the image will be used (publishing, brochure, advertising, etc.); whether it will be used on the cover, interior pages, or the web; the size of the image on the page; expected length of time the image will be used; and so on and so forth. Using a rights-managed image can tend to be expensive and the terms rather limiting, so for convenience and flexibility, as well as affordability, I suggest you purchase royalty-free images.

WEBSITES FOR GRAPHICS AND IMAGES

Inexpensive Stock Photos (Low- and high-resolution files)
www.123rf.com
www.bigstockphoto.com
www.canstockphoto.com
www.crestock.com
www.dreamstime.com
us.fotolia.com
www.istockphoto.com

High-End and Subscription-Based Photo Sites (Low- and high-resolution files)
www.corbisimages.com
www.gettyimages.com
www.inmagine.com
www.shutterstock.com
www.superstock.com
www.thinkstockphotos.com
www.wireimage.com (for celebrity pictures)

Free Photos (High resolution)
www.freeimages.com

Free Photos (Low resolution)
www.flickr.com/creativecommons
www.freefoto.com
www.freephotosbank.com
www.morguefile.com

Illustration and Vector Images
www.illustrationworks.com
www.vectorstock.com

Chapter 4:
Putting It All Together

Managing the Editorial Process

Having created our table of contents, my team and I were lucky enough to know numerous experts and writers to whom we could start assigning stories to right away. We also took suggestions on what stories should appear within what particular topic sections. Since our website had been up and running for over eight years, we had previously been approached by numerous writers and authors who had submitted stories or queries over the years. Luckily for me, I had saved every single one of those emails and so was able to generate content this way as well. We also used our website's chat room and newsletter to solicit other potential contributors.

Our table of contents consisted of three main areas: the mind, body, and soul, and we divided our stories into those particular sections once we had collectively read, evaluated, and approved each one for inclusion in the first issue. The spreadsheet presented in Figure 4 was exactly what I created and used to track the entire editorial process. Due to the color-coding system I employed, I *always* knew the status of every single article at each step of the process.

Figure 4: Spreadsheet to Track the Editorial Process

Order:	TOC Title:	Article Name:
Intro:		
i1	Table of Contents	Table of Contents
i2	Letter From The Editor	Letter From The Editor
i3	Credits	Credits
i4	Holla!	Holla!
i5	New Beginnings	Today I Am A Butterfly
For The Mind:		
M1	Shero	Jacqueline Cornelius
M2	The Queens of Conversation	Spirituality vs. Religion
M3	Through His Eyes	Why Won't He Call Back?
M4	His PRO-file	Ngo
M5	Her PRO-file	Sharona Jones
M6	Artist Spotlight	Georgia Artist
M7	Ask The Harpers	Ask The Harpers
M8	Sister Sound Off	Get Up, Get Out!
M9	Straight Talk!	Your Child vs. Your Man
M10	Wired Woman	The 4 Free Programs Every PC User Should Own
M11	CashFlow	What You Don't Know CAN Hurt You
M12	Carol's Comedy Corner	Forgetting Stuff Can Sometimes Be Hazardous to Your Health
For The Body:		
B1	Work It!	Back To Basics - Jumping Jacks
B2	Your Health	Female Problems
B3	Creating The Balance	Nourishing the Mind, Body, and Soul
B4	HeadQuarters	Split Ends
B5	Fashion Forward	Evolutionary Soul
For The Soul:		
S1	Quiz	How Positive Are You (Really)?
S2	Boarding Pass	St. Lucia
S3	Relations	Opening Up To Love After Being Hurt
S4	Sister Share'on	A Way Out of No Way (Shame And Pain)
S5	Secret Confessions	Confessions of a Stripper
Features:		
F1	Feature	Grief
F2	Feature	Creating Peaceful Spaces
Outro:		
O1	Scopes	Scopes
O2	Crossword	A Tribute To Our Men
O3	SisterPower	SisterPower
O4	Crossword Solution	A Tribute To Our Men
O5	Wind Down Zone	You Are Not Powerless

Description:	Words	Visual	Sign Off	Editing?	Complete	Cover
Table of contents		N/A	N/A	x		
Letter from the editor		√	N/A	x		
Magazine contributors		I	N/A	x		
Reader views and comments		N/A	N/A			
Poetry Corner	198	√	√		x	
Ordinary women, doing extraordinary things	1364	√	√		x	
Queens live chat	2141	I			x	x
Commentary from the male's perspective	1978	√			x	x
Entrepreneur spotlight - Male	931	√	√		x	
Entrepreneur spotlight - Female	726	√	√		x	
Artist spotlight	344	I	√		x	
Relationship advice from Mr. and Mrs. Harper	1439	I	N/A		x	
Commentary page	999	I	√		x	
Reader Q and A	833	√	N/A			
High-tech gadget page	946	√	N/A		x	
Financial advice	1353	√		x		
Carol's comedy corner	700	I			x	
Instructional fitness guide	357	√	√		x	
Women's health issues	1039	I	√		x	
Creating utopia within	743	√	√		x	
Hair and beauty	472	√	N/A		x	
Highlighting the latest styles and fashions	N/A	√	N/A		x	
Quiz	987	N/A	N/A		x	x
Travel page	341	√	√		x	
Focusing on love, sex, and relationships	566	√	√		x	x
Relating the Bible to life today	359	√	N/A		x	
Secret confessions	1032	√			x	
Feature story	1512	√	√		x	
Feature story	1078	√	√		x	
Horoscopes	1366	√	N/A		x	
Crossword	N/A	√			x	
Comic strip superhero	N/A	I	N/A	x		
Crossword	N/A	√			x	
Something to do for next time/Food for thought	300	√	√		x	

I am not sure how other folks do it, but this worked for me. I can't begin to tell you how invaluable this system was. This was the one tool I used to put the whole first issue (and subsequent issues) together. I promise, you are getting your money's worth right here, and hopefully you can use (or modify) my system to track and manage your own editorial process.

Column 1 – Order: This is a column I added in once the first issue was complete, as a guide for story placement when turning over the files to our graphic designer. Although we will ignore this for now, it will be discussed later in Chapter 7.

Column 2 – TOC Title: This listed the title headings of our table of contents. This column was my BIG GUNS, "traffic light" indicator. All assigned stories started off in red. When the completed article was returned, then the color was changed to orange. Once a visual had been assigned *and* the article returned from our editor, then it was changed to green. I cannot describe the feeling I had when all the rows in that column finally turned green.

Column 3 – Article Name: This listed the table of contents subheading or the actual article name.

Column 4 – Description: A description of each title that appeared in the TOC.

Column 5 – Words: The word count of each article.

Column 6 – Visual: This let me know if a visual or photograph had been sourced and assigned to a story. Blank lines let me know that a visual had not been found yet. "I" was used to indicate that a particular visual was an illustration.

Column 7 – Sign Off: Used to indicate whether or not a writer agreement had been sent, signed, and returned.

Column 8 – Editing: As we received stories, they were sent out to our copy editor. The placement of ticks in this column let me know which stories were currently out being edited.

Column 9 – Complete: Once articles came back from our editor, a check would be added to indicate that the editorial process for that article was complete.

Column 10 – Cover: A check mark was added to stories that were to be included as a cover line on the front cover.

Additional Columns: Although not shown here, there were four additional columns: Writer Name, Email Address, Street Address, and Contact Number. This way I always had the information at my fingertips if I ever needed to contact a writer for whatever reason.

I told you . . . INGENIOUS!

The Production Schedule

I just discussed the editorial process without mentioning anything about issue planning, date setting, and the general workflow needed to ensure that your magazine is produced on time. This information will become your production schedule. The deadlines set by your printer or your "on shelf" date will determine all subsequent dates. The production schedule presented here (an .XLS spreadsheet) allows you to enter the "on shelf" date and calculate your due dates backward, according to how many days are needed for each task. Nothing ever goes according to plan, so you must pad in extra days to your schedule and have a backup plan for missing stories, late ads, and so forth. Communicate deadlines to your team so everybody knows who or what departments are responsible each step of the way.

A typical production schedule may comprise the following tasks:
- Issue planning and theme selection
- Cover planning
- TOC planning and review
- Ad prospecting
- Submission call (solicit articles from, and assign stories to, writers)
- Collecting and compiling editorial content
- Issue planning and final selection of stories
- Article editing and visual selection
- Writer agreement distribution
- Article editing and visual selection deadline
- Deadline for writer agreements
- Ad close date
- Finalize magazine page count
- Layout and design
- Design completion (including design iterations)
- Ad soft-copy sent out for approval
- Design check
- Proofreading
- Proofreading complete
- Proofreading review
- Ad approval receipt deadline
- Files finalized, changes checked and entered
- Generation of subscriber labels (for printer)
- Prepress
- Prepress complete (1st round)
- Updated or corrected files back to printer
- Begin the print process
- Print process complete
- Shipper pickup date
- "On shelf" date

Figure 5: Example Production Schedule for a Quarterly Magazine

Department	Deadline	Task	Start Date	# of Days
Staff		Issue planning/Cover planning/TOC planning and review	07/05/17	1
Advertising		Begin ad prospecting	07/06/17	2
Editorial		Submission call	07/08/17	21
Editorial	Deadline	Collect and compile editorial content	07/29/17	5
Editorial		Plan issue/Select final stories	08/03/17	3
Editorial/Art		Article editing and visual selection	08/06/17	1
Staff		Writer agreements distributed and monitored for response	08/07/17	15
Editorial/Art	Deadline	Article editing and visual selection	08/22/17	0
Staff	Deadline	Deadline for writer agreements	08/22/17	2
Advertising	Deadline	Ad art/Ad close/Finalize page count	08/24/17	2
		** PAD **	08/26/17	5
Design		Layout and design	08/31/17	28
Design	Deadline	Design complete (includes iterations)	09/28/17	4
Staff		Design check	10/02/17	2
Proofer		Proofreading	10/04/17	7
Proofer		Proofreading complete	10/11/17	3
Staff		Proofreading reviewed	10/14/17	4
Design		Files finalized, changes checked and entered	10/18/17	0
Circulation		Generate subscriber labels for printer	10/18/17	2
Printer		Files to printer - Prepress	10/20/17	10
Printer	Deadline	Prepress complete (1st round)	10/30/17	2
Editorial/Design		Updated/Corrected files to printer	11/01/17	1
Printer		Begin the print process	11/02/17	14
Printer	Deadline	Print process complete	11/16/17	4
Shipper		Shipper pickup	11/20/17	22
N/A		**"On shelf" Date**	**12/12/17**	

Chapter 5:
Magazine Branding and Design

Your Logo

Like your name, your logo stands for everything your magazine represents and is the cornerstone of your brand. It should be attention-getting, legible, distinctive, and memorable. It's the first thing your reader sees that ultimately conveys a message, mood, and feeling about your magazine.

Your logo should have the ability to be incorporated into everything from business cards to promotional materials and should be made from a custom-designed font that cannot be easily replicated. It can be designed using type only (which is called a logotype), or it can be a combination of a symbol along with typography. Double-check to make sure your logo is legible in black and white only, to ensure its readability in situations where color cannot be produced, for instance with a fax machine—and yes, some people still use them.

Does your logo stand out on the newsstand and differentiate you from your competitors? Ask your designer to create a mock cover to ensure that your logo (which should be located at the top of your cover) can be read from at least eight feet away.

Figure 6: The SisterPower Logo

The Cover

Your cover is the most important page of your magazine, as before it even gets in front of your potential readers, there's the possibility of it being evaluated by distributors, wholesalers, retailers, advertisers, and investors. It's your ultimate selling point, so must immediately grab attention, rouse interest, and successfully communicate your entire magazine's message.

Create catchy, intriguing, benefit-oriented cover lines that entice readers to open the magazine. All available elements such as the logo, image, copy, color, composition, and type must effectively work together to quickly and clearly communicate what your magazine is all about. Using a photograph on the cover is preferred to an illustration. I do not recommend the use of stock photography on your cover, as the image may have already been seen elsewhere. Use an original image and spare no expense in its creation.

Lastly, you should always design your cover with the newsstand in mind. Consumer studies indicate that the cover (along with its design) is the number one factor driving newsstand sales, accounting for 75 percent of single-copy sales.

Figure 7: Example *SisterPower Magazine* Cover

Magazine Layout and Design

When deciding on how your magazine should look, the best thing to do is visit your local bookstore and browse through numerous titles across different categories. Study them carefully, making notes on what you like and what you don't like about them. Combining all the elements you like and avoiding the ones you don't will allow you to create a magazine that has its own distinctive look, style, personality, and character.

Identify different design elements by looking at the following attributes: What are the publication's dimensions? What fonts and font styles are used? Are they consistent throughout the magazine? How large is the type? What about the space between the letters—are words tightly packed or loose? How about the leading (the space between the lines)? How many columns are used? How long or short are line lengths? Is it easy to read? Why? Does the magazine appear light and airy or cramped and uncomfortable? What things make you uncomfortable? Are the left, right, and center page margins wide or narrow? How do they relate to each other? Where do articles and headlines start and finish on the page? How much white space is there at the top and bottom? How are pictures used? Are they bled off the page? How is color used throughout the publication? Is there a specific color scheme? What elements are used to emphasize or de-emphasize sections on the page? Is the magazine graphic-heavy or text-heavy? Do you see a visually cohesive design throughout the magazine?

Being able to identify and answer questions like these prepares you to start communicating with your designer. Take actual magazines, screen shots, or clippings to provide examples of everything you would like to discuss. Ask your designer to create a dummy layout, with three variations, to test whether he (or she) understands your vision and is able to translate your ideas onto paper. This will be a good indicator of whether you have selected the right designer for the job. You may wish to supply an actual article along with image files, although this is not absolutely necessary for initial layout purposes.

Before finalizing your design and editorial formula, it is important to call, talk to, and select a printer (see Chapter 8). Your printer should make recommendations on how best to design your publication based upon the equipment and processes they use in-house. Getting this information up front will allow you to cost-effectively create print-ready files that will require little to no rework on your part. There is nothing worse than selecting a page size of 8.25 x 11.5 and completing the design of 196 pages, only to find out that your printer cannot accommodate this page size and does not support the software the pages were created in. All pages would have to be redesigned in the appropriate software, terribly impacting both cost and production time.

A Word on Typography

During the design process you will have to decide what fonts you will use throughout your magazine to deliver the message. Although your computer comes with hundreds of pre-installed fonts, you only really need two—one for the headlines and one for the body text. Two fonts are sufficient, as a font family may contain numerous styles (italic, bold, extra bold, condensed, etc.) that affect the look, shape, and weight of letters. This allows enough room to provide for both consistency and variety. Although you may deviate and use a special font for impact as a story demands, it is the general consensus that the use of too many fonts does not allow for a cohesive design and can be visually confusing to a reader.

There are two basic classifications of font faces: serif and sans serif. Serif fonts have curlicues at the ends of the letters and sans serif fonts do not. Research shows that serif fonts are easier to read, as the serifs of the letters serve as a guideline for the eye. With that in mind, choose a serif font for your body text, which should ALWAYS be the same leading and point size throughout the publication. Use a sans serif font for your headlines, subheads, and sidebars.

Examples of serif fonts include Times Roman, Baskerville, Garamond, Bodoni, and Palatino. Examples of sans serif fonts include Arial, Helvetica, Futura, Avante Garde, and Myriad.

SERIF FONTS	SANS SERIF FONTS
Times Roman Rilit prat alis ad dolortin utpatue tatem endion ulla consectem dunt prat nim ilisse dolorem.	**Arial** Rilit prat alis ad dolortin utpatue tatem endion ulla consectem dunt prat nim ilisse dolorem.
Berthold Baskerville Rilit prat alis ad dolortin utpatue tatem endion ulla consectem dunt prat nim ilisse dolorem.	**Helvetica** Rilit prat alis ad dolortin utpatue tatem endion ulla consectem dunt prat nim ilisse dolorem.
Garamond Rilit prat alis ad dolortin utpatue tatem endion ulla consectem dunt prat nim ilisse dolorem.	**Futura** Rilit prat alis ad dolortin utpatue tatem endion ulla consectem dunt prat nim ilisse dolorem.
Bodoni Rilit prat alis ad dolortin utpatue tatem endion ulla consectem dunt prat nim ilisse dolorem.	**Avante Garde** Rilit prat alis ad dolortin utpatue tatem endion ulla consectem dunt prat nim
Palatino Rilit prat alis ad dolortin utpatue tatem endion ulla consectem dunt prat nim ilisse dolorem.	**Myriad** Rilit prat alis ad dolortin utpatue tatem endion ulla consectem dunt prat nim ilisse dolorem.

Chapter 6:
Your Marketing Materials

Your Magazine

Your magazine is THE most important marketing piece in your arsenal. Your graphics should be carefully selected to clearly illustrate and convey the right feeling about a story. You should not have to actually read a headline or subtitle in order to get the gist of a story.

Headlines should be compelling and pull the reader in by promising a benefit, arousing interest, or offering helpful information. They should be short and specific and create a sense of urgency that makes the reader have to read, or at least browse, the article right away. Subtitles should elaborate on the headline, giving the reader even more reason to read on.

Your stories should be interesting, informative, unpredictable, and relevant to your readers' interests. Make sure stories are readable and that it is not necessary to pick up a dictionary for every other word. Talk to your reader in a voice and tone they are both familiar and comfortable with. Make your magazine a friend, literally. Hold the readers' attention with each story by taking them on a journey that has a definite beginning, middle, and end. Don't lose them halfway where they think, "What's the point? Why am I even reading this story?" Use fresh ideas and try to add angles and information that have not been explored before. Lastly, your copy should be clean and not contain typos, bad grammar, misspellings, or incorrect punctuation.

Use fonts, color, weight, balance, style, contrast, emphasis, justification, margins, rules, and white space to combine all the above elements into a professional, eye-catching design that effectively attracts and speaks to your reader. Your magazine's appearance should be clean, clear, and readable. Aim to create an identifiable look that stands out and competes with other titles on the newsstand.

The Media Kit

Your media kit introduces your magazine to prospective advertisers and contains all the information they need in order to persuade them to place an ad in your publication. It should get your prospect excited about your publication and ultimately answer the question of why they should advertise with you.

A media kit may contain the following:

A Compelling Cover
An enticing introductory cover page.

Magazine Background and Information
Introduce your title. Who are you? What is your background? What qualifies you to publish a magazine in this field? What is your mission or editorial philosophy? Why is there a need for your magazine? How are you different from other publications out there?

Reader Testimonials

If you have or can generate some, add these to show advertisers the good things people are saying about your magazine.

Press Clips

Include any favorable media coverage you have received thus far.

Reader Profile

Match the target audience with your advertisers. Provide demographic and psychographic information about them, answering questions like: Who are my readers? What is their gender? Age? Family structure (number of children, extended family, etc.)? Geographic location? Education level? Profession or field? Household income? Disposable income? What are their purchasing characteristics? What are their interests? What type of lifestyle do they lead? What kinds of attitudes do they have? What beliefs do they share? How do they spend their spare time? What motivates them?

Circulation

This is the number of readers you have, calculated through the sum of single-copy and subscription sales. Being a new magazine, you will not be able to provide circulation data initially, but you will want to add this information as your magazine grows and the numbers become available. For future reference, official circulation audits are carried out by such organizations as the Alliance for Audited Media (www.auditedmedia.com) and BPA Worldwide (www.bpaww.com).

Market Analysis

Show why you have an attractive market by answering the following questions: What is the size of your target market? Is the market growing, and if so, due to what factors? What is the market growth rate or potential? What makes the market profitable? What are the future trends?

Figure 8: Media Kit - Example Advertising Rate Sheet

Advertising Rates

4 Color

Size	1x	2x	3x	4x
Full page	$5000	$4550	$4050	$3646
2/3 page	$3500	$3150	$2836	$2552
1/2 page	$2626	$2364	$2126	$1914
1/3 page	$1838	$1654	$1488	$1340
1/6 page	$964	$868	$706	$636

Black and White

Size	1x	2x	3x	4x
Full page	$3241	$2916	$2625	$2363
2/3 page	$2268	$2041	$1838	$1653
1/2 page	$3460	$1531	$1377	$1240
1/3 page	$1191	$1086	$964	$868
1/6 page	$536	$562	$506	$456

Premium Positions

Cover 2 (inside front)	$6400
Cover 3 (inside back)	$5868
Cover 4 (back)	$7360
Inside front spread	$9600
Special Position Charge	$400

Marketplace

Marketplace	$550

Send 50 words of copy, along with graphic(s) to marketplace@sisterpower.com. Marketplace ads will be laid out in a standardized format. Please note: The marketplace ads section is subject to omission. If this occurs a 1/6 page display ad will be substituted in its place.

PO BOX 123456, DECATUR, GA 30036 • PHONE: 404.123.4567 • FAX: 404.123.4567 • EMAIL: ADS@SISTERPOWER.COM
W W W . S I S T E R P O W E R . C O M

Figure 9: Media Kit - Example Dimensions Page

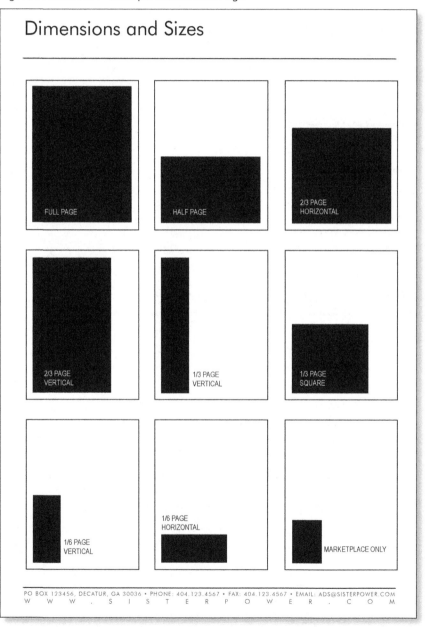

Figure 10: Media Kit - Example Specifications Page

Specs, Requirements and Deadlines

Magazine specifications:

4 color

Magazine page trim size:

8 1/8 x 10 7/8

Binding method:

Saddle stitch

Printing:

Body and covers print web offset

Cover: 100 lb (Sterling ultra with UV coat)

Text: 40 lb

All advertising must be provided in a digital format as follows:

FTP: Contact ads@sisterpower.com for FTP address, username and password settings.

InDesign, Illustrator, Photoshop or Acrobat PDF (300 DPI Resolution, Print Ready).

Photoshop file: CMYK mode (JPG, TIFF or EPS formats only).

CMYK Printing Ink Set-up as SWOP coated, Dot Gain 20%, Total Ink Limit 270°x6.

B/W or color laser proof required to ensure correct information.

Images should be 300dpi/150 line screen. Bitmapped/line art images are 1200dpi.

Original images should be cropped to final size used.

Deadlines:

Issue	Months	Theme	Space Reservation	Art and Payment Due	Mag Mail Date
Winter 2017	Jan-Mar	New Beginnings	Oct 20	Oct 27	Dec 27
Spring 2018	Apr-June	Relaxation	Jan 20	Jan 27	Mar 27
Summer 2018	July-Sept	Relationships and You	Apr 20	Apr 27	June 27
Fall 2018	Oct-Dec	Celebrating Life	July 20	July 27	Sept 27

PO BOX 123456, DECATUR, GA 30036 • PHONE: 404.123.4567 • FAX: 404.123.4567 • EMAIL: ADS@SISTERPOWER.COM
W W W . S I S T E R P O W E R . C O M

Figure 11: Media Kit - Example Advertising Reservation Form

Advertising Reservation Form

Organization: _____

Name of Contact: _____ Job Title: _____

Address: _____

City: _____ State: _____ Zip: _____ Web: _____

Phone: _____ Fax: _____ E-mail: _____

Type of Product(s) or Service(s) Advertised: _____

Reservation

Ad Size	Color or B&W?	Issue(s) In Which Ad Will Appear	Total No. of Ads	Total Amount ($)

Payment

Payment Due Dates:

Winter 2017	September 27, 2017
Spring 2018	December 27, 2017
Summer 2018	March 27, 2018
Fall 2018	June 27, 2018

☐ Check Enclosed   ☐ MasterCard   ☐ Visa   Total Amount Enclosed ($) _____

Credit Card #: _____

Name on Credit Card: _____

Billing Address: _____

Rates are secure for all advertising orders that are contracted for a period of up to 1 year in advance.

Frequency discounts are contingent upon payment in full, for all ads in the series, by the payment due date for the first ad in the series.

Submission of this form to The Publisher constitutes agreement to the following terms and regulations. The Publisher reserves the right to reject or cancel any advertisement, space, position, or insertion order for any reason and at any time, previously accepted or not, without liability. The Publisher reserves the right to mark any advertisement "Paid Advertisement" or "Advertisement" if, in the judgment of the publisher, it looks like editorial content. Advertisers and advertising agencies assume liability for all content (including text, representations, and illustrations) of advertisements printed, and also assume responsibility for any claims arising therefrom. Acceptance of advertising does not relieve advertisers or agencies from liability. Advertiser shall receive the Earned rate plus 10% for guaranteed premium placement on any insertion order, otherwise placement cannot be guaranteed and is subject to revision up until the time of printing. If Advertiser fails to pay the Rates indicated above or otherwise breaches this contract, The Publisher has the right to terminate this contract or modify the Rate indicated above to the most current rate schedule plus 15%. Additional penalties may apply according to contract terms. Refunds are available for any cancellation made within one week after space reservation minus a $50.00 processing fee. Changes to ads are not accepted after the closing date. Ads received after the art submission deadline are subject to postponement.

The Publisher shall not be subject to any liability whatsoever for any failure to publish or circulate for any part of any issue due to strikes, work stoppages, accidents, fires, acts of God or any circumstance not within the control of the Publisher. The Publisher's liability for any error will not exceed the charge for the advertisement in question. The Publisher is not responsible for the accuracy of any corrections or changes made to any advertiser's materials. Rates are subject to change without notice. As used on this advertising reservation form, the term "Publisher" and "SisterPower" refers to SisterPower, LLC.

PLEASE RETURN THIS COMPLETED FORM TO:

_____
Signature

_____
Name (printed)

_____
Date

SisterPower Magazine
Attention: Ad Sales Department
PO Box 123456
Decatur, GA 30036
Office: 404.123.4567
Fax: 404.123.4567
Email: ads@sisterpower.com
Website: www.sisterpower.com

PO BOX 123456, DECATUR, GA 30036 • PHONE: 404.123.4567 • FAX: 404.123.4567 • EMAIL: ADS@SISTERPOWER.COM
W W W . S I S T E R P O W E R . C O M

Editorial Calendar and Highlights
Give information about your content, showing the types of articles that will be featured in upcoming issues. This allows for advertising tie-ins that enable advertisers to determine exactly when to advertise particular products.

Rate Sheet (See Figure 8)
The rate sheet summarizes a publisher's prices for ads of different sizes, colors, and positions; it also summarizes the frequency discounts that are available. (See "Setting Your Ad Rates" on page 172.)

Ad Dimensions and Sizes (See Figure 9)
Graphically illustrate the available ad dimensions and sizes.

Magazine Specifications (See Figure 10)
Describe whether your magazine is black and white or color, the page trim size, approximate number of pages in each issue, binding method, and the type of paper used for the cover and inside pages.

Submission Requirements (See Figure 10)
Let advertisers know what format ads will be accepted in. Examples include PDF, PSD, AI, JPEG, or TIFF files.

Deadlines (See Figure 10)
Let advertisers know space reservation, artwork, and payment due dates for the editorial year. Also include the issue theme and magazine mail date.

Advertising Reservation Form (See Figure 11)
Create an easy-to-understand and fill-out advertising order form.

Staff and Contributor Bios
If it helps to make your magazine look more credible, list some of the main profiles here.

Business Address and Sales Contact Information

Let advertisers know where, how, and whom to contact; you'd be surprised at how many folks actually forget to include this information in their media kits.

The Press Release

A press release is simply a public announcement that is prepared for distribution to various media outlets. It should be concise, informative, and straightforward. A well written release can attract interest, lead to interviews, and help sustain relationships with journalists, editors, and writers. The media needs fresh, credible, relevant news. It doesn't exist just to give you free publicity but to provide interesting stories for their readers. When writing your press release, answer the question, "What makes this story newsworthy?"

You can choose to go the traditional route and distribute your release to editors at newspapers, magazines, radio stations, and television networks. Call them up and find out exactly who your release should be sent to and what department. After submitting a release, always follow up to find out if any additional materials or information would be appreciated. Make sure to have a media kit on hand that is ready to go.

Don't think of a press release as a one-time deal that you only create to announce the launch of your magazine. Find reasons to get in front of potential readers and create news about your magazine as often as you possibly can. Are you holding an event? Receiving an award? Launching a related product or service? Developing an app? Contributing toward a charitable cause? These types of activities all deserve news announcements as they relate to your magazine and serve to bring further definition to your brand and the things that your publication stands for.

PRESS RELEASE FORMAT

A press release should be written in the third person; have a clear, concise, attention-getting headline; and contain two to three brief paragraphs of about 400 words in total. The format of your press release should be as follows:

Dateline
Type the words "FOR IMMEDIATE RELEASE" in all caps. If you wish to release your news on or after a specific date, you can use the phrase "FOR RELEASE ON" and then include the date.

Media contact details
The contact information of the person all inquiries should be directed to. Include name, address, phone number, email and web address.

Headline
This should be in all caps and centered on the page. Use this bold print section to grab the attention of the journalist. It should be catchy, clear, and concise. Think of it as a billboard along the highway. What would you want to say in ten words or less? Communicate the essence of your story straightaway.

Subhead
Elaborate on your headline, giving a little more information. This should be the bridge between your headline and the story. A subhead is not always needed, but if you use one, center the text, use upper- and lowercase letters, and make the text slightly smaller than your headline.

Opening paragraph
Start with your city, state, and the actual date, (e.g., Atlanta, GA, June 2017). Include your most pertinent information, or "the hook,"

Figure 12: Example Press Release

FOR IMMEDIATE RELEASE - JUNE 2017 - CONTACT: CONTACT NAME

Atlanta's Very Own SisterPower.com Launches New Print Magazine

"This has got to be the best I've seen for women of color. Outstanding!!!"
- Celia Treadville

"The magazine is absolutely beautiful. Publications like this make me feel good about myself."
- Denise Somerton

"I just love the magazine. I read every single section and am very impressed..."
- Shirley Crimbley

Atlanta, GA (June 2017) – SisterPower.com has announced the launch of their new publication, Sister-Power Magazine, due to hit newsstands July 1st, 2017.

Priding itself on being the longest running website for women of color, for the past eight years www.sisterpower.com has been the No. 1 destination for African American women on the web. An online support system that was developed to put out a positive message to an often-neglected demographic group on the net, they were able to create a much needed cyber community that immediately forged a bond with (and between) readers.

The publication is visually compelling and editorially stimulating; containing informative, engaging topics of substance, that features "real" editorial, where the majority of content is actually written and submitted by readers themselves. This allows the publication to keep their finger on the pulse of their audience and deliver topics that are relevant and meaningful to them and their life experiences. Dubbed as a manual for women who want to make better choices, SisterPower aims to feed the soul, encourage, motivate and inspire.

SisterPower Magazine is available online at www.sisterpower.com as well as at bookstores and news-stands nationwide.

About the company: SisterPower is a limited liability company formed in Atlanta, Georgia. Founding members are: <Names of Founding Members>.

Please send questions and inquiries to press@sisterpower.com or call (404) 123-4567.

#

PO Box 123456, Atlanta, GA 30036 • Phone:404.123.4567 • Fax:404.123.4567 • Email:sisterpower@sisterpower.com

W W W . S I S T E R P O W E R . C O M

which is the one thing that gets your audience interested in reading on. Pinpoint what is newsworthy about your magazine, giving the who, what, where, when, how, and why.

Body
Elaborate on your story and go into more detail.

Boilerplate
A brief description of the company—history, mission statement, etc.

Final paragraph
Repeat the critical information, your final thoughts, and close out.

Close
End your press release with the standard "###" symbol centered on the page. This indicates that your press release is finished and there are no more sections included.

FREE ONLINE PRESS RELEASE DISTRIBUTION SERVICES

Just perform a Google search for "free press release distribution" to come up with a ton of sites that offer this service. This section includes ones I have personally used over the years and can vouch for. My releases have been published all over the web (including www.usatoday.com) and as a consequence, I received a few interview requests. I even had an offer for an appearance on a major television network, so don't dismiss the power and the amount of visibility an online press release can garner. Also, to your advantage is that your press release will exist in cyberspace for a very long time, if not forever.

Most services allow you to create a free account online but you may consider paying a small fee to upgrade your account for additional features such as the ability to include graphics, embed clickable links into the body of your release, and have your release distributed through that particular company's RSS feed. At a minimum, you should create accounts with, and submit your release to each and every one of the following free services:

1888PressRelease (www.1888pressrelease.com)
24-7 Press Release (www.24-7pressrelease.com)
Free Press Release (www.free-press-release.com)
iNewswire (www.inewswire.com)
Newswire Today (www.newswiretoday.com)
PR.com (www.pr.com)
PRLog (www.prlog.org)
PR Urgent (www.prurgent.com)

Tip: Set up a Google Alert (www.google.com/alerts) to receive a notification every time your press release is featured or referenced online.

The Subscriptions Card

Your subscriptions card is the mail piece that is found on the inside of your magazine that makes it easy for readers to either subscribe themselves or purchase a subscription for a friend. This card can either be stitched or blown in to your magazine.

For readers to be able to subscribe without expense, you should use the business reply mail (BRM) service that's provided by the United States Postal Service. Business reply mail is a direct response vehicle that's used by businesses, publishers, government departments, fund-raisers, and other organizations to seek responses from recipients within the United States (domestic business reply mail) or from around the world (international business reply mail). It is extremely convenient for publishers, as you only have to pay for cards that are actually returned.

Figure 13: Example Subscriptions Card

SUBSCRIBE ONLINE NOW!
www.sisterpower.com

NO POSTAGE
NECESSARY
IF MAILED
IN THE
UNITED STATES

BUSINESS REPLY MAIL
FIRST-CLASS MAIL   PERMIT NO. XX   DECATUR GA

POSTAGE WILL BE PAID BY ADDRESSEE

SISTERPOWER
PO BOX 123456
DECATUR GA 30036-9903

|ₗₗₗₗₗₗₗₗₗₗₗₗ|

Subscribe and Save Now !

☐ **6 Issues** - $24.95

☐ **12 Issues** - $49.90

Name (Please print):

Address:

City / State / Zip

Phone/ Fax

Email - Include address for notification of features, offers and events.

☐ PAYMENT ENCLOSED   ☐ BILL ME LATER

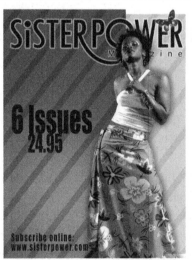

SisterPower Magazine publishes quarterly. Please allow 8-12 weeks for delivery of your first issue. Alternatively, subscribe online at www.sisterpower.com.

The permit fee for Basic BRM–where fewer than 850 pieces are expected to be returned in a year–is $220 per year. In addition to this annual fee, you will be required to pay a small handling fee as well as the price of First Class postage on each piece of mail returned. The current charge stands at $1.17 for each postcard returned. To use the service, you are required to do the following:

1. Obtain a business reply permit
2. Pay the annual, non-refundable fee
3. Design the cards exactly to specification as outlined on USPS' website (free Adobe Illustrator templates for both Mac and Windows are available online).

For complete information, application forms, and templates, go to http://bit.ly/uspsbrm or simply do a search for "business reply mail" directly from the USPS home page (www.usps.com).

Chapter 7:
Production and Your Graphic Designer

Submitting Files To Your Designer

When it's time for layout and design, you will have a collection of files containing all the written articles and visuals you wish to use for your first issue. It will be necessary for you to create some sort of system (or grid) to facilitate the design process, a system that lets you communicate the order of stories, visuals, and ads as they should appear throughout the magazine.

If we refer back to the spreadsheet presented under "Managing the Editorial Process" in Chapter 4, we can use this to facilitate the transfer of files to our designer by modifying the spreadsheet to include only the first three columns. The solid black lines indicate the six sections of our magazine, namely: Intro, For The Mind, For The Body, For The Soul, Features, and Outro. Column 1 (Order) then assigns each section its own set of sequential numbers.

Figure 14: Table of Contents Spreadsheet

Order	TOC Title	Article Name
Intro:		
i1	Table of Contents	Table of Contents
i2	Letter From The Editor	Letter From The Editor
i3	Credits	Credits
i4	Holla!	Holla!
i5	New Beginnings	Today I Am A Butterfly
For The Mind:		
M1	Shero	Jacqueline Cornelius
M2	The Queens of Conversation	Spirituality vs. Religion
M3	Through His Eyes	Why Won't He Call Back?
M4	His PRO-file	Ngo
M5	Her PRO-file	Sharona Jones
M6	Artist Spotlight	Angela Crocker
M7	Ask The Harpers	Ask The Harpers
M8	Sister Sound Off	Get Up, Get Out!
M9	Straight Talk!	Your Child vs. Your Man
M10	Wired Woman	The 4 Free Programs Every PC User Should Own
M11	CashFlow	What You Don't Know CAN Hurt You
M12	Carol's Comedy Corner	Forgetting Stuff Can Sometimes Be Hazardous to Your Health
For The Body:		
B1	Work It!	Back To Basics - Jumping Jacks
B2	Your Health	Female Problems
B3	Creating The Balance	Nourishing the Mind, Body, and Soul
B4	HeadQuarters	Split Ends
B5	Fashion Forward	Evolutionary Soul
For The Soul:		
S1	Quiz	How Positive Are You (Really)?
S2	Boarding Pass	St. Lucia
S3	Relations	Opening Up To Love After Being Hurt
S4	Sister Share'on	A Way Out of No Way (Shame And Pain)
S5	Secret Confessions	Confessions of a Stripper
Features:		
F1	Feature	Grief
F2	Feature	Creating Peaceful Spaces
Outro:		
O1	Scopes	Scopes
O2	Crossword	A Tribute To Our Men
O3	SisterPower	SisterPower
O4	Crossword Solution	A Tribute To Our Men
O5	Wind Down Zone	You Are Not Powerless

I took the files and preceded their names with the order information as found in Column 1. For instance, TableofContents.doc became i1_TableofContents.doc. Graphics that went along with articles were renamed also (e.g., i1_TableofContents1.tiff, i1_TableofContents2.tiff).

For handoff, I created eight folders that stored the files for each section, adding in two extra folders for the front cover and back cover files.

Figure 15: Handoff File Structure 1

If we take, for example, the contents of "5 For The Soul," (Figure 16) we see that the file list corresponds to the TOC spreadsheet, providing the exact order in which stories (and accompanying graphics) should be laid out. The letter "A" was added to advertisement files to indicate their placement also.

Figure 16: Handoff File Structure 2

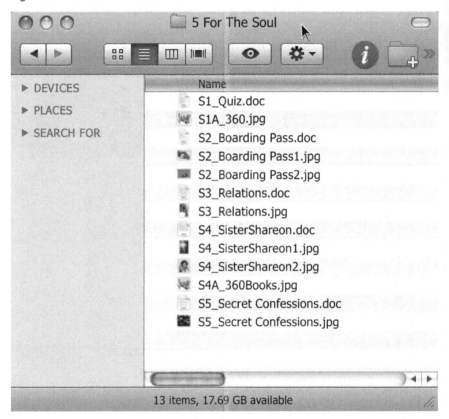

Submitting Articles To Your Designer

To further aid with layout and design, our Word documents were submitted to the designer in the following format:

TOC Title/Section:
TOC Title Name.

Author:
Author's name.

Byline:
Author information.

Headline/Title:
Headline title goes here.

Subhead:
Subhead information here.

Sidebar:
Supply sidebar information (if any).

Pull quote:
Extract possible pull quote information from your main story text in case your designer needs, or can incorporate it.

Main story text:
Story text. Story text.

Prepress

Prepress refers to the process of getting your document ready for print. Although your graphic designer will be responsible for most of this process, it will not hurt for you to become familiar with some of the jargon and activities required at this stage. Most professional publishing software programs have a "preflight" feature that helps package all the elements your printer needs in order to reproduce and print your files correctly. Thoroughly check and recheck your files before submission, as once they are out of your hands, all mistakes will begin to cost you money. Your printer should provide you with a preflight checklist to ensure the smoothness of the job. Here is an example of what your files should be checked for and also what information should be supplied along with your job.

What To Check Your Files For

- Are all files included . . . is there anything missing?
- Can all files be opened? It is a good idea to test this on a different computer to ensure there are no incomplete or corrupt files.
- Is everything labeled correctly?
- Have all original images and graphics been supplied?
- Are they in the correct format?
- Have all images been converted from RGB to CMYK?
- Is all artwork supplied in high resolution at 300 dpi or higher?
- Have you identified, embedded, or included all the fonts for the job?
- Are page settings correctly specified?
- Have document file bleeds been set correctly?

Information to Supply Along With Your Print Job

- Complete contact information
- The type of job

- Expected turnaround time and job completion date
- Total price quoted
- Amount paid
- Balance to pay
- Quantity to be printed
- Page size
- Total page count
- Cover paper type and finish (coated or uncoated)
- Inside paper type and finish (coated or uncoated)
- Information on inserts or special pullouts to be included. Are these to be blown in, bound in, or glued in? What page number(s) should they appear on?
- Whether you are using either B/W, two-color, four-color, or spot color printing
- The type of binding to be used (saddle stitch or perfect-bound)
- Shipping details
- Special shipping or bulk shipping details
- The platform that the files were created on (Mac or PC)
- Name and version of the software the files were created in
- Names and descriptions of all the document files included
- The names of any special software plug-ins used for the job
- A hard copy printout of your entire project, page for page, so your printer knows exactly what your project should look like in advance. Some printers only require a soft copy PDF version but going over a hard copy together will not hurt and can serve as a point of reference for both of you later on down the line.

Once you submit your files, it is now your printer's job to get everything ready for production and identify any potential problems such as missing or corrupt files, graphics that are still in RGB mode, or any problem fonts. They will either tell you how to fix the problems yourself or how much they will charge to fix them for you. If you decide to do it yourself, then resubmit your files, including all the fixes.

Once your files have been successfully transferred and there are no more errors, then it's time to generate a proof.

A proof is a printout that should resemble, as closely as possible, the final printed piece. It is used to check that all text, graphics, and colors look as expected before going to press. This is where you will go through your magazine with a fine-tooth comb, correcting any errors you may find. Fixing errors at this stage can be costly and possibly delay the original estimated turnaround time.

Proofreading Your Proof

Once you have your proof in your hands, proofread it very slowly and carefully. If you receive a soft copy proof make sure to print out a hard copy of the document as it's been proven that the way we read from a screen is very different to the way we read on paper. No matter how many times you have already read, proofread, and edited your document, once the magazine is laid out in its final form, it is likely that you will still find errors that were previously missed. Boldly notate and circle any discrepancies you find. Have your staff members read through and supply corrections, too. It's also a good idea to have a fresh pair of eyes look over your final layout, so you may wish to hire a professional proofreader to give it the once-over as well.

In addition to the visual notations, compile a list containing all the page numbers and accurately describe the problems. This will serve as proof of everything you outlined to your printer before going to print. Once your list is compiled, discuss all the changes with your printer. Ask questions about anything that doesn't look right to you. Don't let a possible question turn into a printed mistake. Here is a list of items to check on your proof:

- Check that page numbers appear in the correct sequence, in the correct location, and on the correct pages

- Check that the page numbers in the table of contents correspond to the correct page numbers throughout the book
- Examine headlines, subheads, photo captions, and display type for correct information, wording, typos, fonts, spacing, and placement
- Read stories out loud, checking for misspelled words, typing errors, missing or broken words and sentences, and incorrect punctuation
- Check for extra spaces and blank lines throughout the text
- Check column spacing and alignment
- Check the gutter spacing on all pages and spreads (this is the white space that is formed by the inner margins of two facing pages)
- Check that graphics are scaled and cropped correctly; that they appear in the correct places, with the correct stories; and that they exhibit colors as expected and are not blurred or out of focus
- Check for miscellaneous page smudges, spots, lines, or other stray markings that may reproduce in print

Once the final proof has passed your inspection and all corrections have been made and approved, YEA! you are ready to print.

Chapter 8:
Working With Printers

Selecting A Printer

This is going to be one of your most vital relationships, so make sure you pick a printer with caution. Call the print shop and ask to speak to someone in sales. Explain your print needs and gauge how receptive they are to your new project. I had a couple of printers die with laughter when I told them I wished to print 8,000 copies, so make sure your printer is someone who you are comfortable with and takes your project just as seriously as you do.

When selecting a printer, look at how long they take and how thoroughly they respond to your emails or messages. Do they provide brief, presumptive answers, or are they detailed and explanatory? Do they sound bored and robotic or enthusiastic and excited? How quickly are your calls returned? How important is your project to them? Do they care as much as you do and take the time to address your needs and concerns? All these factors will help you with your decision. This is a partnership (and maybe even a friendship) that you will need to create in order to ensure great quality and service in the final production of your magazine.

Other key pieces of information to help you determine the right printer for your needs:

Printer specialty

Printers have various specialties. Don't take for granted that just any old print shop can print your magazine. Magazine printing calls for certain equipment, skills, and disciplines, so your printer must have adequate magazine printing experience. Ask who their current customers are—printers are usually proud to tell you who they are working with. Check print samples from previous jobs and make sure these appear satisfactory to you. Check for durability, quality, and for text and color reproduction. Pay special attention to the trimming, making sure pages are straight, do not appear lopsided, and have not been trimmed too close to the content.

Location

There are many printing services offered online. Although going this route may seemingly be more convenient or less pricey, it is not a practice I recommend for a first-time publisher. Nothing beats being able to actually meet with your printer, the staff, and tour the facility. Being able to watch the equipment in action, smell the paper and ink, and see the printed pieces at various stages of production is not a process any publisher should deprive themselves of. It's exciting to know that one day soon your publication will be on those very presses.

By using a local printer, we were able to cut costs tremendously. Although print costs for a company in Colorado were virtually the same as for our local print shop, once we factored in the shipping costs to Georgia, those prices rose dramatically. Also, it was convenient to be able to pick up and deliver our proofs. The whole experience was just more personal and we were able to deal with problems much quicker since the plant was literally just minutes away.

Printing equipment

Do they use a web or sheet-fed press? A sheet-fed press is much slower and more expensive than a web press. Make sure the print shop has the appropriate equipment for your job, taking into consideration the quantity to be printed, number of pages, document size, and type of paper required.

Turnaround time

This is the complete time it will take for your printer to produce your magazine. Most print shops will take, on average, from about one to three weeks to complete the entire process. Be sure that the time given is in line with the requirements of your production schedule. Add in extra time for any unexpected delays that may occur during this process.

Computer platform

Do they use Mac, Windows, or both?

Supported software

What software and version numbers do they use in-house? Do not presume that because they have InDesign that you will be able to print there. Double-check the version number just in case they are using an older version than what you are. Of course, submitting a PDF file will eliminate the need to perform this step or the step above.

Environmentally-conscious practices

"Green printing" is printing in a way that is friendly to the environment, using natural inks and recycled, chlorine-free papers and practicing energy conservation methods. If you are concerned about the environment, find a printer who uses environmentally responsible printing technologies and practices.

Choosing Your Paper

If you are starting out like I was, then I suggest that you check the magazines in your local bookstore and look at the different types of paper available there. You will begin to notice the differences in brightness, thickness, look, and feel. Bring samples to your printer, then they will be able to advise you on the best paper choices based on what is available and the relative prices.

Let your printer know that you are new to the business and need all the help and advice you can get in order to print as cheaply as possible, without too much sacrifice to quality. Look at their print samples, which will be in the form of magazines, brochures, booklets, etc. Ask to see their "house stock." This is the paper your printer buys in large quantities, enabling you to save money as it is already in-house and does not have to be specially ordered and shipped specifically for your project.

There are two main classifications of paper—coated and uncoated. Uncoated paper costs less and is easier on the environment than coated paper. This is what often appears on the inside of a magazine and is referred to as either "book" or "text," along with its weight number.

The weight of the paper most often used for magazines is 60# (pronounced "sixty pound") and would be referred to as "60 lb text." Heavier weighted sheets cost more per sheet than lighter sheets, so the higher the paper weight, the more expensive it is.

Paper is also classified in grades, ranging from grade 5 at the lower end to grade 1, which is premium stock. Grade 3 is pretty standard for magazines. Low-graded paper is more likely to contain recycled fibers than your premium stocks that appear bright and flawless. In addition, low-graded paper does not handle four-color printing very well, but if that's the effect or style you want, then it may work for you.

Your cover will usually be printed on a heavier weight than the inside pages, ranging anywhere from 60 lb to 110 lb. If you would like the cover on the same paper as the inside, then specify to your printer that you would like your magazine printed with a "self cover." Once again, you will select whether your cover should be coated or uncoated, and there will be various choices for coating, such as varnish, aqueous, or UV, depending on your budget and desired result. Ask your printer to recommend an appropriate cover weight, according to your text choice, binding method, and the number of pages to be printed.

Magazine Binding

Your magazine will most likely either be saddle stitched or perfect-bound. Saddle stitching is the fastest and most economical binding method where the leaves are secured through the center fold by wire staples. The process does not actually use manufactured staples as we know them, but creates the staples from a spool of wire that is cut by a machine and stitched into the printed pages, which are draped together over a saddle-like holder. This binding method can be used on magazines that are 100 pages or less, although the actual amount will depend on your paper thickness. Anything bigger will result in the center pages "popping out" or coming away from the center fold.

Perfect binding is adhesive binding that is used for larger publications. With this method the printed pages are shaved along the side and glued at the spine. A cover is then added that encloses the pages and is also held in place by glue along the inside spine.

Preparing For A Print Quote

To receive a quote it will be necessary for you to describe your job specifications—providing clear, accurate information. The quote will usually be valid for 30 days and will include an estimated price, turnaround time, proposed schedule, and information on the type of proofs to be used for the job. Ask your printer what changes in specifications would result in either cheaper printing or a faster turnaround.

Provide information as follows:

Contact details: Contact name, email, website, billing address, phone number, fax, and mobile number.

Type of job: In this case, it would be a magazine.

Publication date: The date your magazine will be released or available to the public.

Frequency: How often will you publish? Weekly, biweekly, monthly, quarterly, etc.

Quantity: How many magazines would you like printed? Ask for two or three quote variations. In my case, I asked for the job to be quoted at 8,000, 10,000, and 12,000 copies. It was interesting to see that due to economies of scale, printing 4,000 more copies resulted in only a $1,700 difference. Note that due to the spoilage that can occur during the printing process, printers often produce within 10 percent more or 10 percent less of the actual amount ordered. Your invoice will be adjusted to reflect this print overrun or underrun. If you absolutely need a specific amount, outline this requirement in your specifications.

Binding method: Saddle stitch or perfect-bound.

Page size: The norm is 8.5" x 10.75". Depending on your printer, finished sizes other than this standard may result in higher prices. If necessary, find out what size variations you can use according to the equipment your printer has.

Self cover or plus cover: Specify whether your magazine is self cover or plus cover. If the cover is going to be made from the same paper as the inside pages, this is a "self cover." If you plan to print the cover on a different paper than the inside, this will be a "plus cover."

Page count: If opting for a self cover, include the cover as part of the total number of pages. Quoting "fifty-six pages self cover" would result in an actual total of fifty-six pages, including the cover. If opting for plus cover, then DO NOT include the cover as a part of the total page count. Instead, quoting "fifty-six pages plus cover" would actually result in a total page count of sixty pages—fifty-six interior pages plus four pages for the cover. When deciding on your page count, please note that magazines are printed on large, oversized, single sheets of paper that allow for eight (or sixteen, depending on the paper and press size) pages to be printed per sheet. This signature is then folded, collated, glued or stitched, and trimmed. Taking this into consideration, you should plan for your magazine's total number of pages to be in page increments of eight (or sixteen). Check with your printer for exact requirements.

Any inserts or special pullouts to be included: For instance, subscriptions cards that may be blown in, bound in, or glued in.

Cover paper type, weight, and finish: For example, "Cover: 70 lb. Gloss Text." (Specifications can include coated, uncoated, varnish, aqueous, UV, etc.)

Cover paper ink: B/W, two-color, four-color, or spot color printing (this is where specially mixed inks are applied individually on the printing press.)

Inside paper type, weight, and finish: For example, "Text: 40 lb. #5 Gloss Text." (Specifications can include coated, uncoated, gloss, matte etc.)

Inside paper ink: B/W, two-color, four-color, or spot color printing.

Delivery method: Will you pick up the finished magazines from your printer, or will you have them shipped? If they are to be shipped, let your printer know the city and zip code they'll be delivered to so delivery charges can be reflected in your estimate.

Shipping details: Find out what shipping services your printer provides. Some printers provide mailing services that ship your magazines directly to subscribers or distributors. If your printer does not provide this service, then you will either have to do it yourself or find a business that specializes in mailing and distribution (or logistics) services.

Computer platform files were prepared on: Mac or PC.

Name and version number of the software files were created in: This ensures that your printer carries the same software you are using, or at least a compatible version of it.

Format the files will be provided in: Native files in their original format or generated PDF files.

How files will be delivered: Files will usually transferred over FTP or by online services that allow for the transfer of large files such as Dropbox (www.dropbox.com), WeTransfer (www.wetransfer.com), and files2U (www.files2u.com). Although rare, some folks may decide to personally deliver or mail in their files on CD or DVD.

Print Quote Example:

Here is the document I received back from a printer a few days after submitting my quote request:

Figure 17: Example Print Quote

Sales Proposal
Subject to Terms, Conditions and
Trade Customs on attached sheet
Estimate #:8888888

For SisterPower Magazine
Attn: Lorraine Phillips

Subject: Sister Power Magazine   Frequency 4 X

Trim Size: 8.125 X 10.875

Page Count: 80 Pages + Cover

Preparation: Client to provide disk with PC or Mac PDF files for direct to plate imaging to Printer's specs. A
                Sample disk is requested for review prior to job submission. Printer to provide Oris color
                proofs and folded Impress proofs for review prior to printing Any work not specifically itemized
                in this proposal are additional at current rates

Paper: Cover: 70lb. Gloss Text   Text: 40lb. #5 Gloss Text

Ink: Cover: 4/4 + Varnish   Text: 4/4

Finishing: Saddle-Stitch

Shipping: Carton Pack with Local Delivery

Quantity: 8,000....................................$11,272.00
Price:,   10,000..................................$12,127.00
               12,000 ....$12,977.00

The above proposed pricing does not include the State of Georgia sales tax. Verification of Tax Exemption is required. The Enclosed pricing is
good for 30 days. If credit terms have not been established then: Terms 50% in advance and the balance due prior to shipment.

Accepted:

Printer Reps Name
Printers Address   *By:*_____*Date:*_____
Printers Name

PART II

Creating an Online Presence

Chapter 9:
Your Magazine's Website

Why You Need A Website

I'm pretty sure that in this day and age there isn't anyone who needs convincing on the importance of having a web presence. But just in case— here are just a few reasons why your magazine needs a website.

1. Provides the most cost-effective promotional sales and marketing tool available that allows you to promote your magazine 24/7, worldwide.
2. Establishes brand credibility.
3. Allows you to clearly demonstrate your magazine concept and editorial philosophy.
4. Increases visibility and allows you to be found in search results for both content and images if labeled correctly (see Chapter 12) .
5. The ability to accurately track analytics and find out what types of content have been most popular with readers so you can see what works and what doesn't.
6. Helps to locate potential contributors to your magazine.

7. Allows for direct communication with your audience through newsletters, polls, surveys, and questionnaires.
8. Allows you to collect both demographic and psychographic data on your audience.
9. Can grant subscribers exclusive access to bonus content on your site.
10. The ability to set up an FAQ page that can immediately answer frequent customer queries or questions.
11. The ability to market and sell promotional items—hats, T-shirts, water bottles, bags—to further increase brand awareness.
12. Showcases your media kit to prospective advertisers.
13. Provides a chance to offer additional discounted or free advertising opportunities on your site to current magazine advertisers.
14. Allows you to generate extra income by accepting ads that can be featured either on your site or your newsletter.

Also worth mentioning here is although we know that social media is a powerful tool for marketing and building relationships with your audience online, it's of the utmost importance that you have your own "home" that you totally own and administer, that exclusively demonstrates your magazine and brand, and is the hub of all your online marketing efforts. When you use a social network you are in a sense just renting space from them—they have all the control and impose terms and limitations as they please. (Think of owning your own home versus renting an apartment.)

Say, for instance, Facebook (or another network) changes a rule tomorrow, much to the discontent of its users who, as a result, decide to leave in droves. That can be an entire audience you automatically lose as you have no real control over that platform.

What Your Website Should Contain

Your website should be based on audience needs and set up in a way that makes it easy for visitors to browse and subscribe to your magazine.

You should feature compelling, relevant, useful content that is updated regularly—no one is going to return to hear the sound of tumbleweeds. Web communities are formed when users are engaged and entertained. Make it as interactive as possible by giving readers things to do. Supply content that encourages conversation and allows them to comment and provide feedback. You can also provide links from the content to a discussion board or social network so readers can connect, interact with each other (another important factor), and share ideas and information. At a minimum, your site should contain the following:

About Us

Introduce your magazine, discussing your mission, concept, reason for being, or any other pertinent information that visitors may find interesting. Use language that gets them excited about your publication.

The Table of Contents (TOC)

Make your current TOC easy to view. Never force a user to download and open a file to look at your TOC.

Magazine Content Preview and Highlights

Display a sample of your magazine's content. Make sure to feature and highlight links to your most popular content.

Back Issues

Give visitors a place where they can view, purchase, or download back issues of your magazine.

Subscriptions

Create a simple sign-up form where readers can easily and conveniently subscribe online. Make the form (or subscribe link) prominent throughout your site.

Stockists

Give the addresses of places where your magazine can be purchased either online or offline. For offline stockists make sure to include both national and international vendors.

Writer's Guidelines

Describe what kinds of articles you are looking for and exactly how they should be submitted (See example in Chapter 3).

Contact Us

Provide a contact form where readers can send their comments, feedback, or enquiries. A contact form is a better choice because it protects your email address from exposure as opposed to a link, which can be easily picked up by "spam bots" and used to send spam email.

Frequently Asked Questions (FAQs)

Provide a page that answers your most frequently asked questions like what to do if an issue is damaged or how to change a subscriptions address.

Ratings, Reviews, and Testimonials

Let visitors know all the good things people are saying about your magazine. Try to update these comments on a regular basis.

Advertiser Page

Create a page specially dedicated to advertisers that provides direct contact information to your ad sales team, including names, phone numbers, email addresses, and links to social media accounts. Also, make sure to feature a downloadable PDF media kit.

Newsletter Sign-Up Form

Create a space or page where readers can easily sign up to receive information via newsletter. This gives you the ability to collect email addresses and communicate directly with your audience. Keep them informed by sending out a monthly digest of your best content, relevant and interesting news, pertinent developments, information on events you may be holding, and any contests or special offers you may have. Your newsletter should contain enough interesting information that makes a reader want to click through to your site and further explore what's found there. Increase trust and your readers' willingness to divulge email information by including verbiage on the form similar to "This information will be used for correspondence only. We respect your privacy, and your email address will never be shared, sold, or rented." And of course, follow through with your promise. Also, remember to include an "opt-out" link in your newsletter as a courtesy should readers decide not to receive further emails. For email marketing services, you can check the following companies: AWeber (www.aweber.com), Constant Contact (www.constantcontact.com), iContact (www.icontact.com), and Mad Mimi (www.madmimi.com).

"Follow Us" Buttons
Provide links to all your active social network accounts. (The key word here is *active!*)

Social Media Sharing Buttons
Incorporate buttons that allow users to easily share your content with their personal networks on Facebook, Twitter, Digg, StumbleUpon, and others. AddThis (www.addthis.com) and ShareThis (www.sharethis.com) provide code, widgets, and plug-ins that allow you easily to add this feature to your site. Both services also provide analytic data that lets you see exactly where and how your content is being shared.

Search Capability
Readers like having the ability to search for specific information (possibly due to our Google habits), so don't miss out on providing this valuable tool on your site. Incorporating this function will also allow readers to search through and find articles from archived copies of your magazine.

Survey

You can set up a survey to collect data on your readers that can be used to provide information for advertisers in your media kit. Gathering this information also allows you to tailor your website and magazine to satisfy audience needs. Speak your audience's language and keep it as simple as possible. Add a disclaimer to let readers know that their information will be kept confidential. It may read something like: "This information provides us with feedback so we can better serve your needs. All information provided will be kept confidential and not be disclosed or sold in any way." SurveyMonkey (www.surveymonkey. com), Typeform (www.typeform.com), Wufoo (www.wufoo.com), and Zoomerang (www.zoomerang.com) all offer a free basic service (you will have to purchase a plan to unlock the more advanced features) that allows you to create web-based surveys for your audience. It may be worth offering some type of incentive to encourage readers to fill out the form.

Note: Having a survey or questionnaire on your site, although valuable, may be considered the "old-fashioned" or outdated way of collecting information as with the advent of social media, you can now poll, question, and contact your audience in real time.

Ancillary Products

You can sell products or services in addition to the magazine to raise awareness and generate additional income. Examples of such products or services include creating special industry reports; holding events, workshops, or seminars; selling books, videos, or training materials; or selling promotional items such as T-shirts, hats, and bags.

Games and Entertainment

Give your visitors something fun and relaxing to do. Get them "addicted" to your site by including additions such as horoscopes, polls, and quizzes. Aim to keep them hooked and coming back for more.

EXAMPLE SURVEY QUESTIONS

- What is your full name?
- What is your email address?
- What state or country do you live in?
- What is your gender?
- What is your age?
- What is your highest level of education?
- What is your current occupation?
- What is your average annual household income?
- What is your marital status?
- What is the number of dependents in your household?
- What magazines do you currently subscribe to or read?
- What is your primary method of purchase for these magazines? (i.e., newsstand, subscription, etc.)
- How did you hear about this magazine?
- What section of the magazine do you enjoy the most?
- What section of the magazine do you enjoy the least?
- What would you like to see more of in this magazine?
- What do you like most about our website?
- How often do you visit our site?
- How often do you visit or participate on our social networks?
- Do you primarily use the internet for personal, social, or professional needs?
- What types of products do you purchase most often online?

Chapter 10:
The Set Up

Choosing Your Host and Registering Your Domain

Your host's function is to store your website, or the pages you create, on its servers and display those pages over the web. Your registrar is the company through which you will register your domain name. Your host and registrar can be one and the same, or they can be different; it's entirely up to you. If you decide to purchase a hosting plan from a provider that is different from your registrar, then your host will give you the instructions on how to "point" your domain to its servers so that you can physically host and administer your site with them. Either way, it's a quick and easy process to complete.

Over the years, I have built websites for clients using many different host providers, and the one I can highly recommend is Just Host (www. justhost.com). Their hosting plans start at $2.95 per month, and the features offered just can't be beat. You get a free domain for life (so no extra cost is involved if registering a new domain); unlimited website space (which means that if you need to upload a trillion videos, you can); unlimited streaming or data transfer; unlimited email accounts; free WordPress, Joomla, and osCommerce installation; and worldwide 24/7 technical support that includes live chat. If that wasn't enough, there is also an anytime money-back guarantee.

Just Host provides a simple, intuitive user interface (or control panel) that you use to administer your site. Also, when you purchase a plan, you receive unlimited domain hosting, which means you can host multiple domains on a single account. So you'll never have to buy another hosting plan no matter how many websites you decide to build in the future.

If you are not ready to purchase a plan but would still like to secure your domain name, then I suggest registering over at Cosmotown (www.cosmotown.com), who tout themselves as providing the lowest cost in domain ownership and so far, I have found their claim to be true. Hunt around for coupons online as the internet is always rife with discount codes you can use for the service. Here are my eight rules for selecting a domain name:

- It should preferably be a dot-com.
- It should be exactly the same name as your magazine. If that's not available, then choose something that's extremely close (maybe by popping "mag" on the end for clarity).
- It should be as descriptive as possible and provide a clue as to what your magazine is about.
- It should be reasonably short.
- It should be catchy, easy to remember, and easy to pronounce.
- It should not contain any underscores, as links are often highlighted or underlined, making a URL that contains an underscore somewhat hard to read.
- You should not use hyphens unless you absolutely have to, and even then, your address should not contain more than one. As in the case of a site called Who Represents (www.whorepresents.com), they might have been better off purchasing the hyphenated version so

that the address would be much easier to decipher and read as www. who-represents.com.

- It should not be confusing or difficult to find (i.e., not the .net or .org name of an already existing, established, well-known .com site).

Why You Should Hire a Designer

Unless you are truly familiar with web design principles, a master at computer languages (e.g., HTML5, CSS, Ajax, and PHP), and a skilled graphic designer, then I do not recommend that you attempt to build the site yourself.

Web design covers many disciplines—which evolve daily—and it will take a considerable amount of time to learn each one as well as learn how to integrate them all successfully. Forget picking up any of those HTML5 for Dummies-type books. You should be fully emerged in the process of putting your magazine together, so I highly suggest that you hire a professional for the job.

Professional web designers specialize in presenting information (or content) in a way that is functional, efficient, and aesthetically pleasing. Your site must be built around audience needs, so make sure it is easy for readers to navigate and find information quickly. We've all visited those hideous, frustrating sites—never to return again, which is exactly what we don't want to happen here. Hire a designer who has the skills, knowledge, and experience to implement the pages and features you desire. If you don't know of any professional designers personally, then check the freelance resources available online. Hiring a professional designer can help you avoid the following web faux pas:

- Nonbranded, inconsistent, incohesive design
- Slow-loading pages and graphics
- Unclear navigation where users cannot easily recognize what page

they are on or identify where they need to go

- Nondescriptive navigation that does not clearly communicate the information contained on each page
- Frustrating menus that function incorrectly
- A website that is not targeted toward a particular audience (e.g., a site aimed at teens should look different from a site aimed at retirees)
- Important pages (such as the subscriptions page) buried too deep within the site, making it difficult for readers to find relevant information quickly
- Browser incompatibility, where your site displays and acts differently depending on which browser, browser version, platform, or device it is being viewed on
- A design that is not optimized for mobile devices
- The use of fonts that are not available on all computers, resulting in the site looking different depending on which platform or device it is being viewed on
- Not using effective SEO techniques
- Not including social media sharing functions
- A cluttered design
- Overuse of annoying, blinking, or flashing banner ads or graphics
- Lack of contrast or use of an unpleasant color scheme
- Hard-to-read text due to choice of background color, text size, or text color
- Orphan pages that do not provide a way back to the originating page, forcing users to click the browser's "Back" button (which is a big web no-no)
- Broken links that either do nothing or lead nowhere, resulting in the "Page Cannot Be Found" error message
- Vertical scrolling (another classic no-no)

Questions to Ask Your Designer or Web Design Firm

If you decide to hire a web designer, you will need to ask the following questions:

Is there an online portfolio I can view?

Most designers showcase completed projects online. Check to make sure their work exemplifies the style, flair, and design characteristics you are looking for. It will be great if they have had experience developing other online magazines. Make sure to use my web faux pas checklist to evaluate their level of competency.

Will I be able to handle site updates myself?

The answer to this question will vary according to what solution your designer decides to implement for you and what web skills you possess. If this option is important to you, then say so at the onset of the project to make the designer aware of your needs. With content management systems (such as WordPress and Drupal) that allow for easy updating by non-tech savvy users, this should not be a problem, but updating a custom-made website will be much more labor intensive and will require you to know a little HTML and possibly CSS too.

Will pages be optimized for search engines?

It is important that your designer understands how to structure pages in a way that works best for SEO.

Will the site be mobile-friendly?

Your website should be optimized for mobile reading so that it can easily be viewed on smaller screens and devices. Mobile-friendly sites include features such as large buttons; simple, thumb-friendly navigation; easy-to-access search functions; and a limited amount of pinching, scrolling, and zooming needed in order to view content. Ask for examples of the designer's most recently designed mobile-friendly sites and view them on a variety of devices (such as your desktop, tablet, and phone) to ensure that viewing on all devices result in a positive user experience.

This feature is extremely important as Google has announced that preference will be given to results that identify as being mobile-friendly websites for searches performed from smartphones or tablets. Sites that don't fit the description will consequently be demoted in search results. Although this formula will not affect searches performed on desktop or laptop computers, when you think about it, Google would not be performing its duty if it displayed results that were totally useless to mobile users. Lucky for us, Google has provided a tool that can analyze and test whether your site is indeed mobile-friendly and provides both pointers and directions for those that are not. You can find the tool at http://bit.ly/googlemfriendly.

Can you set up and area, page, or widget that will make it easy for browsers to subscribe to the magazine?

Provide your designer with a list of the type of information you need to capture from the subscriptions page for your database, such as name, address, phone number, email address, date of subscription, subscription length, amount paid, etc.

Can you set up a "members-only" section of the website?

There are various options and scripts available online that will allow for members-only access to predefined content on your site. Ensure that your designer is familiar with the process and is able to implement this solution if required. (If implementing this feature in WordPress see Appendix B for a list of recommended plug-ins.)

Is it possible for you to implement newsletter sign-up, survey, or contact form scripts?

Scripts should be set up to send all information directly to your email address. Have your designer create an autoresponder that automatically sends a confirmation email to the recipient's address. If it's an enquiry from your contact form, don't take long to respond. Having a reasonably fast response rate is an important feature of your site that lets visitors know that you are actually there (in real time) and that you care.

Can you make it easy for users to share information with their social media networks?

Expand your audience by ensuring that social media sharing buttons are set up on your site. Have your designer suggest viable options for doing this or simply discuss the sites AddThis (www.addthis.com) and ShareThis (www.sharethis.com) with him or her.

What information will I need to provide to generate an estimate for the entire project?

Please see the next section of this chapter entitled "Information You May Need to Provide." Know that you are responsible for the accuracy of the information supplied; it is not your designer's job to correct spelling or fix bad grammar.

What will be the approximate cost?

Submit requests to at least three designers for price comparison. Even better—if you use an online freelance provider service, designers will bid at competitive rates for your project.

What are the payment terms?

All design shops function differently, but you will receive a proposal or estimate that is usually valid for thirty days, based on the project specifications and the anticipated scope of the work. When you approve and sign off on the estimate, you will usually need to deposit at least 50 percent of the total amount, with the balance due upon prototype sign-off (as discussed below).

How long will it take to complete the design?

This will depend on the complexity of the project and your designer's anticipated workload at the time.

What is the usual development process? What checkpoints and milestones will there be along the way?

After you sign off on the estimate, pay the deposit, and supply your designer with all the information needed, he or she will create either a prototype web page, a sketch, or a printout that demonstrates the general page layout of your site. In the case of a prototype, actual functionality will not be implemented until later on in the process. The sample layout will demonstrate the colors, fonts, navigation, buttons, logo and graphics placement, and any other design-related elements that are pertinent to the project.

What happens if I do not like the design?

If, as you work with your designer to refine the design, you just can't seem to see eye to eye and he or she seems incapable of implementing your ideas, then it will be necessary for you to cut ties and pay the money owed thus far. If you take time to find a designer who comes with a recommendation, matches your style, and has produced work you are impressed with, then this scenario should not arise.

What happens if I decide to cancel the project?

This will depend on how far along in the process you are when you decide to cancel the project. Charges for services rendered may be 25 percent to 50 percent if the work is canceled during the initial design phase, 50 percent if canceled after the completion and sign-off on the prototype, and 100 percent if canceled after the final design is complete.

How are revisions and alterations handled along the way?

If the revisions or alterations are deemed within scope, as according to the original proposal, then they are already included as part of the estimated fee. If developments require new items or functionality that are deemed out of scope or were not defined within the original estimate, then a new proposal and estimate will have to be generated.

How is website compatibility testing handled? What browsers and platforms do you test on?

Your website should be tested to ensure it acts and looks the same regardless of platform, operating system, browser, or device used. At a minimum, insist that your site be tested on both Mac and PC and a couple different mobile devices as well as in various browsers, including Firefox, Internet Explorer, Google Chrome, and Safari.

Will you provide tech support? If so, for how long?

Most designers will offer free technical support for anywhere from seven to thirty days after your site goes live, providing an opportunity to work out any minor quirks, bugs, or tweaks you discover. Use this period to thoroughly go through your site to ensure that it functions and displays exactly as required.

Information You May Need to Provide

Here is some of the information you may need to provide to your designer in order to receive an accurate estimate and timeline for your website design:

- What is your magazine's name?
- What is the tag line or slogan?
- What is your editorial philosophy? Why do you exist?
- Who is your target audience?
- What are the goals and objectives of your site? (See overleaf)
- What is the desired theme, style, or appearance of your site? For example, are you hip, funky, professional, feminine, conservative,

trustworthy? Find a few adjectives that describe your style or brand.
- Number of pages the website will have?
- What are the website's main subject categories?
- What are the names and descriptions of the pages that will appear in each category?
- Will you include any special site features or functionality such as a subscription sign-up area, newsletter sign-up form, or social media sharing capabilities?
- Provide the URLs of three websites you like and three you don't. Tell your designer what you do and don't like about each one.
- What are your preferred colors? Supply color samples for accuracy.
- Are there any colors that should absolutely not be used?
- What materials do you plan to provide (i.e., logo, images, articles)?
- What is your desired date of completion?

EXAMPLE GOALS AND OBJECTIVES FOR YOUR SITE

- Increase awareness about the magazine
- Showcase magazine philosophy, content, and design
- Ensure site is mobile-friendly
- Allow for subscription sales (add a "Subscribe Now" button to every page on the site)
- Drive action (encourage user actions such as increase newsletter subscriptions or donations)
- Use viral marketing (or social sharing) techniques that make it easy for users to inform others about the site
- Build a community
- Communicate with advertisers (downloadable media kit)
- Conveniently collect survey statistics

Chapter 11:
Your Magazine's Blog

WordPress CMS

A content management system (CMS) is a software tool that allows for the creation, editing, publishing, distribution, and discovery of electronic content such as text, images, graphics, video, sound, and documents. A blog constitutes a CMS, and it enables a user to freely and easily publish content to the web, through a web-based interface, with no official technical knowledge or training necessary. This is the primary reason why blogs are so popular and in such widespread use today.

A magazine's blog will differ from that of a traditional blog. A blog is typically defined as being the personal platform of a single author who has a particular interest or point of view on a specified subject, and is written in a conversational tone. A magazine blog will differ in its approach to content creation and delivery in that there will be several contributors who publish according to a set schedule, providing varied content that is centered around a basic theme. The most distinguishing fact between the two is that quality control (which can include fact-checking, researching, and correcting errors in grammar, syntax, punctuation, and spelling) is performed on all content by an editorial staff.

There are several content management systems available online but with over 75 million installations of the software worldwide, WordPress is rated as the number one content management system on the web today. The software is freely available for download, and if you already have a domain name and web host (as the software requires installation on a web server), it can easily be installed to your website. Check with your host for details as it is literally a one-click set-up process.

WordPress' number one rating is due in large part to the unlimited number of add-ons, plug-ins, themes, tools, and features available, giving you the flexibility to both create and grow your magazine's blog any which way you may need to in the future. Depending on your specifications and feature requirements, you may need to hire a developer or designer who can customize and brand your site with an appropriately tweaked theme (or create one from scratch) as well as install the various plug-ins and widgets you may require. If you decide to do it yourself, there are numerous tutorials and step-by-step guides available online that can show you how to carry out most of these functions on your own.

Note: For a list of "Essential WordPress Plug-ins," please see Appendix B.

Selecting a WordPress Theme

A WordPress theme, or template, will allow you to create the design, look, feel, and structure of your magazine's blog. There are literally thousands of themes available online, and the process of selecting one can be both time consuming and overwhelming. The following criteria should help make the process of selecting a theme a little easier for you.

1. Ensure the template you select works with the latest version of WordPress. Visit www.wordpress.org for information on the most current release.

2. If possible, steer away from WordPress themes that are available for free as they often contain encrypted code in the footer section of the template that is protected from editing and if tampered with, can stop a site from working altogether. If a free theme is downloaded from an obscure website, then there is also the risk of it containing malicious code that can end up being disastrous for a site.

3. Choose a theme that is flexible and has the most customization options. Keep in mind that you will probably want to tweak your magazine's blog by either adding more functionality or changing its structure later on down the line.

4. Confirm that the theme is SEO friendly, has plenty of SEO features, and will work with major plug-ins (such as WordPress SEO by Yoast) to ensure your site's visibility on the web.

5. Ensure the template is "widget ready." Most widgets enable a user to customize theme sidebars according to layout needs by adding functionality, such as listing the most recent posts, the most popular posts, or displaying relevant ads.

6. Make sure the theme includes social media integration with "Share" buttons that show alongside content. Other considerations may be "Follow" or "Like" buttons and the ability to display your Twitter or Facebook stream.

7. Go for a responsive, fluid, adaptive theme that automatically adjusts to a visitor's screen size and allows your website to display perfectly on any device.

8. Check the license to find out whether you receive free support, if you are entitled to unlimited updates at no extra cost, whether there's a money-back guarantee, and if there are any restrictions associated with the use of the template.

POPULAR THEME PROVIDERS

There are numerous reputable websites where you can purchase and download themes online. The following companies are considered to be amongst the most popular and reputable theme providers.

Elegant Themes (www.elegantthemes.com)
Press75 (www.press75.com)
Solostream (www.solostream.com/wordpress-themes)
StudioPress (www.studiopress.com)
Templatic (www.templatic.com)
Themeforest (www.themeforest.net)
WooThemes (www.woothemes.com)

Blogging and SEO

It's a well known fact that search engines just love blogs. Topic-specific, regularly updated blogs are rewarded by Google and other search engines with higher page rankings. As Rick Bruner, former research director of DoubleClick, put it, "Blog stands for Better Listings On Google." Frequently updated content means that spiders return regularly to re-index your content and ensure they always have the latest, most current information from your site.

"The squeaky wheel gets the grease," as they say, so people searching for information on your particular subject matter will find you more quickly through a regularly updated blog than they would through a static website that does not have a blog or is not frequently updated. Always use carefully selected keywords for your post's title, body text, tags, permalink (which is the URL that points to a specific blog post after it has passed from the front page into the archives), as well as the names of any graphics, audio and video files, or link text you incorporate as we will discuss in Chapter 12.

Another advantage a blog has over a static website is the ability to receive "trackbacks." A trackback is an automated alert that is sent to a blog owner to let him or her know that a particular post has been linked to or referenced from another site. Most blogging software supports trackbacks. According to the settings of the particular platform, a trackback sends the name of the site that's referencing it, the URL, the title of the post, and a short excerpt of the contents. What's really great about this is that a trackback will automatically create a comment on the original post that was referenced; this comment provides a link to the new post, giving readers the opportunity to discover blogs within the same subject category, which can result in an increased amount of incoming traffic for the blogger who made the reference. Linking to, or referencing, posts from other blog sites that appear within your niche can be used as a technique to get your publication noticed. It can also serve as a method for creating an abundance of inbound links–but make sure your readers are truly benefiting from the information that you link to and share.

> **Tip:** For an easy way to generate links and get help with SEO, link the main keywords in your blog post to other relevant documents on your site at least once within the body text. Although internal linking is not as important as links from external sites, it still helps. When linking this way, make sure to use the full URL, including the "http://" part of the address.

Ideas for Blog Promotion

Here are a few ideas you can use to promote your magazine's blog:

- Ensure all blog posts are SEO friendly
- Incorporate email subscription capability

- Include social media sharing buttons for networks such as Facebook, Twitter, Pinterest, Instagram, and Google+ to make it easy for readers to share content with their networks.
- Announce your best and most relevant posts via email and on Facebook, Twitter, or other social networking sites. If posting to Twitter, use the hashtag symbol as it relates to your subject matter (e.g., #beautytips).
- Bookmark and tag your best articles on sites like Digg (www.digg.com), Delicious (www.delicious.com), reddit (www.reddit.com), and StumbleUpon (www.stumbleupon.com).
- Search for questions on Twitter and LinkedIn that relate to your particular subject and respond by presenting links to meaningful blog posts or articles on your magazine's site.
- Participate in other communities. Visit related forums, groups, and blogs to leave feedback or answer questions, linking to posts or articles from your site that relate to the question at hand.
- Network and build relationships with popular bloggers and magazines in your field who already have established audiences. After a relationship is established, ask for links to your content.
- Widen your audience by having some of your writers guest post on other blogs or magazine sites. Always include a link back to your magazine's blog in the byline.
- Use Google Analytics to find out which sites are sending you the most traffic and consider building relationships with them.
- Find out who is linking to the popular blogs in your subject category by going to Google and typing in "link:www.the-blogs-name.com." Use the list to generate inbound links by promoting your magazine's content to these sites using the methods discussed thus far.
- Add your magazine blog's URL to your email signature, business cards, website (if separate), press kit, press releases, brochures, flyers, and any other promotional materials you may have.

Note: I do not advise syndicating your blog content across all social networks and announcing every single post or article you create, as people who follow you across several networks may view this behavior as somewhat "spammy." Instead, I suggest you only post your best, most relevant, and most valuable content to your other networks.

Measuring Your Blog's Success

Everybody will have different criteria, according to their desired goals, for measuring a blog's success. Potential advertisers will also be interested to know the following information, so make sure to include it as part of your media kit after your traffic picks up. A blog's success can be measured by any of the following:

- The number of visits
- The number of visitors
- The number of new visitors versus the number of returning visitors
- The number of page views per visit
- How long visitors stay engaged on the site
- The number of comments received
- The quality of comments received
- The general feedback received
- How many people are citing and linking to your blog
- The number of "shares" you receive to (or from) social networks
- The number of newsletter sign-ups
- Search engine rankings
- The number of magazine subscriptions that came as a result of your blogging activities. (Note that if you are performing numerous online marketing activities then the results from one particular effort can be hard to determine or track without the use of a specific URL or purchase code.)

Chapter 12:

Preparing Search Engine-Friendly Web Pages

Understanding SEO

Now it's time for us to get a little technical. There's no point in being on the web if you can't be found and search engine optimization (SEO) is the official term for improving the visibility, or rankings, of a web page in search engine results. Search engines work by sending out automated programs, called spiders or robots, that crawl the internet, visiting sites, reading the information found there, and then indexing this information by storing the results in a database. Crawlers refresh these indexes at different intervals, periodically returning to sites to check for updated content. Storing the data this way allows for quick searches online; otherwise, bots would have to physically crawl the internet every time a search is performed. I couldn't even begin to imagine how long a method like that would take today.

Considering that 80 percent of traffic to a website comes through a search engine, it is imperative that as a magazine publisher, you understand the principles presented in this chapter. Making your website search engine friendly simply means that a web page has been coded in a way that makes it easily accessible to these crawlers—explicitly and clearly providing the specific information they look for, as well as presenting that information in the best possible manner. The primary method used by search engines for finding, indexing, and cataloging a site is by keyword which we will discuss over the following pages.

KEYWORD RESEARCH STRATEGIES

Your job is to find the most common phrases used to search for your particular subject matter and include those terms as keywords on your web pages so that you might rank higher in search results for those terms, thereby increasing your chances of actually being found on the web. When creating your list of keywords, try not to be too general. Remember, you are competing against a ton of other websites out there, so it's important that you zone in on specific search terms and phrases.

Never use one-word keywords, as this will guarantee that you don't get high rankings. For instance, if your magazine focuses on the subject of golf, don't just use the word "golf" or "golfing" as a keyword. Instead, use phrases such as "perfecting your golf swing," "how to align a golf shot," "golf swing training," or "free golf instruction guides."

When researching the best keywords to use for your particular niche, take "long tail keywords" into consideration. Long tail keywords consist of three or more words that are the less common, less competitive keywords searched for but that can be responsible for delivering significant levels of high-quality, targeted traffic to a site. For instance, the specific phrase "Canon PowerShot Digital Camera," as opposed to the more general "digital camera," indicates that the searcher knows exactly what he or she is looking for and is probably ready to take some type of action, whether that means making a purchase, signing up for a newsletter, or downloading a report. Focusing on less popular terms can also increase your site's chances of being highly ranked for your selected keyword phrases.

To clearly define what your audience searches for—just as you did when planning your magazine and researching the competition—spend some time browsing the web, visiting similar sites and their corresponding social networks. Take note of the types of topics discussed and the kinds of words and phrases used, making sure to jot down any recurring themes you find. Plug these phrases into a keyword research tool to see what other keywords or phrases you can come up with. If using Google AdWords, you can also plug your URL, or a competitor's URL, into the website field for a list of suggested keywords. Then compile a list of keyword phrases that you find that are not too competitive and appear most consistently across results.

KEYWORD RESEARCH TOOLS

Free Services
Google AdWords (www.adwords.google.com)

Paid Services with Free Trials
Keyword Discovery (www.keyworddiscovery.com)
SEMRush (www.semrush.com)
Wordtracker (www.wordtracker.com)

To go into more depth regarding the actual keywords that a competing site is using, enter any of the keyword phrases from the list you have now compiled into your favorite search engine and note the sites that show up in the top set of results that closely match your content offerings. Head over to ABAKUS Topword (http://bit.ly/abakustopword) and enter each of the URLs you have found there too.

This amazing tool analyzes the top keywords in a web page, providing you with a list of the most used single keywords, two-word phrases, and three-word phrases that can be found on a page. Once again, look for similarities and differences between these results and what you have already found. Using the information you have already compiled, create a final master keyword list that consists of at least six to ten phrases you can use as target phrases on various pages or articles throughout your site.

It is important to know that search engines read web pages from the top down. Aim to place your keyword phrases at the very top of the page (if you can, before the main header or navigation), and toward the front of the first set of paragraphs. (Think headline, headline, headline; and yes, subheads too.) Continue to sprinkle your phrases throughout the content or text on your page.

The main pages of your site should be optimized for at least one specific search term, with your home page being optimized for your most important keyword phrase. This strategy allows the pages in your site to rank for several keyword terms (instead of just one), and it also eliminates the possibility of pages within your site competing against one another for particular search terms.

Always ensure that your content is packed with information in a way that makes it relevant, unique, interesting, and useful to a visitor. Don't try to stuff so many keywords into a page that your content becomes nonsensical. Although you're aiming to make your pages search engine friendly, your first order of business is to ensure that your pages are readable and make complete sense to your audience. If they are unable to make heads or tails out of what they're reading, then they won't be visitors for long and will definitely not return.

Attempting to overstuff content with keyword phrases (and other questionable SEO tactics, such as attempting to hide keywords by making your text color the same as the color of your background) is known as "black hat search engine optimization," and is generally frowned upon by most search engines. Using techniques like these can get a site completely removed from search results for good.

USING KEYWORDS WITHIN GRAPHICS

You should also place your keywords in the image descriptions used to display graphics on a web page. In HTML, the **<img>** tag is used to embed, or place, an image on the page. Because spaces are not accepted within file names, hyphens are preferred. Here's an example:

<img src="graphics/volkswagen-golf-hatchback.jpg"/>

In the statement above, the "**src**" attribute stands for "source," and it supplies the name of the image while defining its location on the server relative to the current document. This image is called "volkswagen-golf-hatchback.jpg" and can be found in the "graphics" folder.

Devising and creating descriptive file names in this way provides much more information to a search engine than an image named, say, "IMG00023.jpg." Descriptively naming your images also increases the chances of them showing up for appropriate searches in engines like Google Images, giving searchers yet another way to possibly run across your magazine's site.

Always make sure to fill out an image's description. In HTML this is done using the "**alt**" attribute (note that the WordPress field for this value is called "Alt Text"). The information presented in the "**alt**" tag is indexed by search engines to also help determine a page's relevance for rankings and Google has officially confirmed that it mainly focuses on the information provided as alt text when trying to understand what an image is all about. It's handy for a user too, as alt text provides alternative information for an image in the form of words displayed in place of a graphic if in case that graphic is not displayed for some reason. Here are some of the many reasons why a graphic may not be displayed on a screen:

- A user has his or her graphics turned off
- There is a slow connection

- The user is using a text-based browser such as those found on Unix and Linux systems
- The user uses a screen reader, which is a talking browser for the visually impaired

With that in mind, it's a good idea to combine your keyword phrase with an accurate description of your image, which should be no longer than five words maximum. An effective use of the "**alt**" attribute may be as follows:

<img src="graphics/volkswagen-golf-hatchback.jpg"
     alt="Volkswagen Golf Hatchback Car"/>

PLACING KEYWORDS IN TEXT LINKS

When search engines come a-searchin', they also crawl and analyze the text links found on your site, so it's of the utmost importance that these links be relevant, descriptive, and once again, contain your keyword phrases. Because text links stand out on a page, they are actually given higher priority and more weight than any surrounding text. Knowing this, you should never have worthless links that simply read "Click Here." Provide a clue as to what you're linking to with links that read "Click Here for (fill in the blank)," where the blank contains your relevant keywords.

PLACING KEYWORDS IN DOCUMENT TITLES AND URLS

When naming files, documents, and URLs, make sure to include keywords in the titles you create. Examples of good file names to use on a golf site might include the following:

Golf-swing-tips.html
Golf-swing-instructions.html
Golf-swing-training.html
Improving-your-golf-swing-report.pdf
Improve-your-golf-instructional-video.mp4
Golf-tips-from-the-pros.mp3

Link Building and SEO

Another factor to take into consideration when trying to up the ante in search results is the relationship you have with other websites and the number of inbound links you receive from them. Search engines presume that if you have a lot of sites linking to you, then you must be providing valuable, resourceful information. Algorithms measure both the quantity *and* quality (whether they come from reputable, important, high-ranking sites) of incoming links with the goal of rewarding high-quality websites that provide for a "good user experience."

Don't be tempted to participate in any of the "1,000 Backlinks for $9.99" type programs. You don't know where those links are from, what reputation the sites have, and whether any of them are blacklisted. Unnatural links from shady, questionable websites used in an attempt to manipulate Google (or any other engine) can negatively impact your rankings regardless of what other SEO techniques you employ.

In addition, search engines also check the relevancy of your inbound links. If your site's subject matter is basketball, it won't help you in the least to have a backlink from a dog grooming company's website, so stay away from backlink services where you have no control over who will be linked to you. I advise that you concentrate on creating great content, and the rest will take care of itself.

When adding outbound links from your site, make sure they highly relate to your website content and will further enhance your users' experience. To check the number of inbound and outbound links to your site, you can use Open Site Explorer (www.opensiteexplorer.org), which shows a detailed view of the page as well as the domain authority of incoming links. Use this tool to also see what sites are linking to your competitors, as these will be sites that you can possibly pitch and market your magazine to as well.

Chapter 13:
Being Web Savvy

Submitting Your Site to Search Engines

We have all seen the "We will submit your site to 75,000-plus search engines and directories for the low price of $29.95" offers. But come on, think about it—what 75,000 search engines and directories do you know of that exist? At most, I can recall about five, and evidently they are the only five I really need to know. So even if this claim is true, it is definitely overkill!

These days, search engines are so good at finding and indexing websites that it is no longer necessary for you to do the process yourself by manual submission or through a service. Diehards and control freaks like myself, and especially those who have a new site under a new domain name, should visit Free Web Submission (www.freewebsubmission.com), where you will find direct links to the top fifty highest ranked search engines and directories that you can submit your site to. It can take up to a week before you see your site show in search results. If you wish to carry out the process yourself—or are "old school" like me—then just submitting to the following three services will suffice:

Bing (www.bing.com/toolbox/submit-site-url)
Dmoz Open Directory (www.dmoz.org)
Google (www.google.com/addurl)

Note: Yahoo! submissions now take place through Bing, so submitting your site to Bing means that you are submitting to both.

Monitoring Your Site with Google Analytics

After your site is showing in listings and has been up and running for a few months, it's a good idea to check your web statistics to determine how well your site is performing by analyzing how visitors are interacting with it. Google Analytics is the most popular and widely used tool for this purpose, providing statistical data in the form of graphs and reports you can use to gauge site performance. On signing up for an account (accounts.google.com) and registering your site, you will be provided with a tiny snippet of JavaScript code that will need to be installed across all pages so that you can track relevant statistics. If using a content management system such as WordPress, then you will need to add the code (once) directly into your template or theme. Alternatively, you may use the Google Analytics for WordPress plug-in or Google Analytics by Yoast.

Monitoring site statistics will give you insight into what works and what doesn't so that you might improve your content offerings, site design, features and functionality, marketing initiatives, or keyword selections. (See "Keyword Research Strategies" in the previous chapter.) This information will also help you decide what activities you need to continue focusing on, increase, or possibly eliminate altogether. Find out who visits your site, from where, when, what search terms were used, how long visitors stayed, what path they took, what pages were most popular, and what pages your site was most commonly exited from. This is also some of the information that digital advertisers will be interested in and these statistics can be included as a part of your media kit. In particular, you should pay attention to the following statistics:

Traffic Sources

Find out the top sources of traffic to your site so that you can measure the effectiveness of your marketing activities. What websites are regularly sending traffic your way? Are most visitors coming to you via search engine or social network? Which ones in particular? Monitoring this stat will provide you with the answer.

Keywords

This statistic monitors the keyword phrases or terms visitors used to search for and find your site. Look at these results to determine whether your targeted keywords are accurate and pages delivered matched the information visitors were looking for. High bounce rates for a term (which occur when a visitor leaves a site after viewing a single page) can indicate that the page was not relevant and did not meet expectations. This statistic can also provide hints as to what additional content you may need to provide.

Total Visitors

This statistic lets you see how many different people visited your website within a fixed time frame, usually hourly, daily, weekly, or monthly. If the same visitor visits your site on January 1st and then again on January 3rd, then that visitor would be counted twice as a daily unique visitor and once as a weekly or monthly unique visitor.

New vs. Returning Visitors

If there are a high number of new visitors to your site, then you can determine that you are being successful in driving traffic to your site. If there are a high number of return visits, then you can determine that readers are finding your content engaging, relevant, and useful.

Mobile

This shows the number of visits that came from a mobile device (including tablets) and what those devices were (e.g.,Apple iPad, Apple iPhone, Samsung Galaxy, and HTC Sapphire).

Page Views (or Unique Page Views)

This shows which pages are most popular on your site, indicating what readers are finding most valuable or entertaining. This statistic can be used to see whether changes to certain pages result in more visits or what kind of content you need to provide to keep visitors engaged.

Click Path or Visitor Path

This statistic shows the sequence of hyperlinks followed or the actual path a visitor took while browsing through a website. Following this statistic can help you understand why visitors come to your site and what they look for after they get there.

Landing Pages

Landing pages are the most popular pages upon which visitors enter a site. The more relevant the page, the less likely a visitor will be to bounce or leave right away. If you notice high bounce rates on certain pages, try to analyze why (i.e., determine what source the traffic came from or what keywords were used) and assess what functionality or content you need to add or change to satisfy expectations.

Exit Pages

This statistic shows the last page a reader visited before leaving your site. If you notice a high dropout rate on a certain page, then you may consider updating the content or simplifying the design. Although results are not conclusive, this statistic, when used in conjunction with the click path or visitor path, may reveal what pages users find least useful, boring, or confusing.

Visit Duration

This statistic shows how long visitors spent on your site (in increments of seconds) and how many pages they viewed in that time. Depending on the type or function of your website, you will have different ideal targets for this statistic.

Conversions

A conversion is defined as the number of visitors who complete a desired action beyond just surfing and perusing your site. Desired actions could be purchasing a subscription to your magazine, signing up for a newsletter, or downloading a file. This statistic, when set for the particular action you would like to measure, allows you to determine just how well your site is fulfilling its business goals.

Using Social Media Listening Tools

Social media listening tools allow you to search, track, and analyze conversations that are happening on the web in real time. This can be extremely valuable in finding out who's talking about you (or your competitors) and exactly what they're saying—good, bad, or indifferent. Here are some ideas of what you should be listening for on the networks:

Your magazine's name: Who's talking about you? What are they saying? How are you generally being perceived in the market? On what social networks or sources (blog, news site, etc.) are you being talked about? Who and where are your advocates and key influencers? Whenever possible, actively respond to readers and thank them for their comments and interest. If what readers say is not that positive and you feel their comments warrant a response, then acknowledge the feedback by thanking them for their input and for bringing their concerns to your attention. Let them know that you are always looking for ways to improve your publication and that this is something you will be working on in the future. Some folks may just be acting plain old mean. They are called internet trolls and it may be best to ignore them, but otherwise learn to use negative comments in a positive way.

Your URL: When monitoring your URL, do not add "www" to your search query, as most people will simply leave that part off. Find out who's directing folks to your website by sharing your URL and why.

The names of competing or similar magazines: Track both the names and URLs of other magazines in your genre. Although you've already researched these magazines, you'll want to keep abreast of their latest developments, which includes staying on top of how their audience continues to respond to them.

The central topic(s) upon which your magazine is based: Keep up to date on the buzz of what's happening within your industry so that you can effectively respond, participate, and be in the know. Staying current is extremely important for any publication. You can plan editorial content around breaking or developing news. Better yet, if you're the one who's breaking the news and creating the buzz. Use this technique to find potential readers for your magazine by setting up queries for your most important keyword phrases and seeing who's having conversations on the topic. Depending on the network being used, you may have the ability to chime in right away. If you think an article or a section of your magazine could be of value, then make the user aware of it and point them in that direction. You should be an expert on your subject matter and have the ability to strike up conversations regarding the specific information, possibly letting them know that you currently work for "X" magazine and feature that type of content on your website and in your publication.

The magazine industry as a whole: It is important to stay updated on the latest trends within the industry, as the field (much like everything else nowadays) is in constant flux. What innovations or breakthroughs are taking place? Who are the latest successes (or failures) and why? What new software solutions or services are being developed that can help you streamline your process and help you create a better experience for your readers? Monitoring the industry as a whole will help to provide you with some of these answers.

Note: See Appendix A for a list of links to industry news and resources.

SOCIAL MEDIA LISTENING TOOLS

There are numerous tools and services that can perform the function of social media listening. Find a list here of the more popular free tools available. As will be indicated, some of the sites also provide a more robust paid version of their services.

Google Alerts (www.google.com/alerts)
As previously mentioned, Google Alerts can be set for weekly, daily, or instantaneous alerts on the subjects of your choice. Results consist of Google search results and are sent directly to your email.

Hootsuite (www.hootsuite.com)
Hootsuite is a social media management system (not just a listening tool) that allows you to manage and post to multiple networks such as Twitter, Facebook, LinkedIn, Google+, and WordPress through a secure, web-based dashboard. You can schedule posts, upload images, shorten URLs, and create custom reports using the comprehensive set of social analytic measurement tools provided. The listening portion allows you to search Twitter for mentions, keywords, and hashtags. Hootsuite comes in both free and paid versions, with the free version allowing you to register and administer up to five social media accounts.

Ice Rocket (www.icerocket.com)
Specializes in blog searches and does not require account registration.

Social Mention (www.socialmention.com)

Social Mention is an easy-to-use search and analysis tool that aggregates content from a wide range of sources around the web into a single stream of information. You can select to restrict results to certain social networks or, for example, to only query microblogs. Social Mention also produces statistics on your search that include sentiment (whether the responses were positive, negative, or neutral), top keywords, top users, passion (the frequency of mentions by the same authors), and sources. Results can be saved as .CSV Excel files, email alerts can be triggered, or you can choose to set up an RSS feed.

Figure 18: Topsy Comparison Search

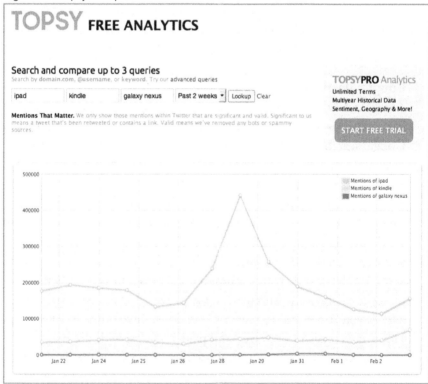

Topsy (www.topsy.com)

Topsy currently offers three services on its website, namely Social Search, Social Analytics, and Social Trends. Social Search gives real-time insight into relevant conversations that are taking place on the web. Unlike the other tools, Topsy uses an algorithm that indexes and ranks results based upon the most influential conversations it finds on the web. The advanced search lets you drill down enough to construct very specific terms that can be found within a site, domain, or a particular Twitter user's stream. The Social Analytics portion allows you to search and compare up to three queries at a time (for instance, the iPad, Kindle, and Galaxy Nexus as shown in Figure 18). A graph shows all the Twitter mentions received over a given time period, and a table is presented with three tabs that contain the links to mentions received in the last twenty-four hours. Social Trends allows you to track the trends across links, tweets, photos, and videos. Topsy comes in both free and paid versions.

Chapter 14:
Social Media

Creating a Strategy

Social media has forever changed the way that people connect, communicate, discover, and share information online—and it provides a free, efficient tool that publishers can use to market their titles online. With Facebook at over a 1.35 billion active users, YouTube at over a billion, Instagram at over 300 million, and Twitter at 288 million, that's a lot of eyeballs, and it will be your job to find your target audience of potential readers and build relationships with them by engaging them with useful, relevant, informative, entertaining content.

To use social media effectively, it will be necessary for you to create a plan that's integrated with your overall marketing strategy so that you create a cohesive (magazine) brand and user experience. Don't just jump out there without a clue as to your purpose or a clear understanding of what needs to be communicated, on what networks, and to whom. It's imperative that you understand your audiences' needs. A reader is always going to be asking themselves "What's in it for me?" (better known as WIIFM) so you'd better have an answer that's strong enough to make them become loyal followers, readers, and maybe even subscribers.

The first thing you'll want to do is define your goals for using social media as a marketing tool. What is it exactly that you want to accomplish? Do you want to raise awareness of your magazine, establish yourself (or your magazine) as an expert or authority in the field, increase website traffic, build loyalty, develop a community, acquire a load of fans and followers, or boost subscription sales, etc.? Having a set of objectives will help you prioritize and determine the necessary steps you need to take to accomplish your goals. These objectives also provide relevant indicators that can help you measure just how well you're doing.

Next, you will need to find out what's important to your readers. From the research you have done thus far, especially after having undertaken your keyword research strategies, you already have a good idea of what subjects and topics your audience is interested in talking about. Also, don't forget to use social networks to poll your audience to receive firsthand knowledge on the subjects they'd like to read or discuss and also use the networks to get feedback from your audience so that you can gauge your performance and find out what you need to do to improve efforts and keep them satisfied.

Know that true (and real) communication consists of 50 percent listening and 50 percent talking. Listening is going to be the single most important skill for you to practice when using social media effectively, and it should be carried out on a continuous basis so that you can find out and keep up with exactly what's important to your readers and create engaging two-way (I repeat, two-way) conversations from there. The rule is (just as your mother taught you) listen first, then talk.

After you've defined your goals and researched your audience and your competition, it's time to decide what type of content and information you plan to share. What do you think your audience will find most valuable? To develop engaging, relevant content, think of things that people want, or things that motivate them. Going back to our list from Chapter 3, examples include the following:

- To be liked and appreciated
- To find love and commitment

- To build a strong self-image
- To achieve better health and longer lives
- To lead more fulfilling lives
- To be more attractive to the opposite sex
- To attain financial security and wealth
- To be entertained and have fun
- To find solutions to their problems
- To know how to save time and be more efficient
- To gain knowledge or expertise on a particular subject
- To learn how to perform a task
- To receive buying advice on products and services
- To be self-sufficient, including owning their own business
- To understand their place in the overall scheme of things
- To gain clarity and direction
- To be motivated and inspired
- To find inner peace
- To be successful
- To express themselves by sharing personal stories and experiences

Think about how often you plan on communicating with your audience and what networks you intend to use. Where do you think you can most likely and easily connect with the potential readers of your magazine? What networks will be most appropriate for your content? For example, Twitter is great for short bursts of information (tweets are 140 characters or less) or for publishing links and teasers to articles, while Facebook is ideal for telling stories and having real conversations with your audience. YouTube is wonderful for showcasing video, and Pinterest and Instagram are great for telling stories visually. A study conducted by ROI Research found that 44 percent of respondents are more likely to engage with a brand if the company posts pictures than any other media, so keep that in mind as you make decisions on what networks you will use.

As you create your various accounts across the networks, remember to include your most important keywords within your magazine's profile description. Make the information presented there both interesting and descriptive, as well as searchable. Be sure to include a link that points readers to the most important page of your website. Brand pages on sites like Facebook, Twitter, Google+, and Instagram by prominently displaying your magazine's logo and including compelling cover images.

When posting information, never aim to overtly (and annoyingly) sell you magazine. Social networks are primarily about being social and providing value, so encourage conversation by regularly posting interesting and relevant content. Good content allows for interaction and dialogue, and it should spark conversation not only directly with you (the magazine) but between the members of your audience as well.

Spice up your posts with real-time news updates, links to articles, links to content from other providers (become a resource), sneak previews, interesting photos and videos, behind-the-scenes stories and footage, inspirational quotes, games, polls, quizzes, coupons, occasional contests, and special offers that are exclusive to your subscribers. Always use language that is both natural (no jargon allowed) and conversational. Be an active participant and regularly respond to comments to keep the conversation going. Don't let any of your accounts resemble a ghost town. If you're not regularly hanging out and having fun, then your readers won't either.

As your magazine gets underway and you begin to work out the kinks that will inevitably be involved in the creation process, I recommend that you start out using no more than two social networks and graduate from there. Don't give up too soon, however—social strategies are not short-term strategies, and just like offline relationships, building lasting relationships with your audience online will take time. Be both patient and consistent. As long as you stay dedicated, relevant, and authentic, your efforts should pay off over time.

Regularly review Google Analytics (but not obsessively) to see which networks are sending the most traffic to your website or use the analytic tools supplied by the social networking sites themselves to see what types of content or communications garnered the most response. Refine (or adjust) your social media strategy according to the results you find and the insights that you gain.

Magazines to Observe

The following sections present a diverse set of magazine brands that are faring exceptionally well across the social networks. They have large, extremely engaged followers, and there's a lot to be learned from them. Closely study each one; check their strategies to see how you can best leverage the networks that you plan to use.

FACEBOOK

Facebook (www.facebook.com) is the number one social network and the second most visited site on the net, runner-up to none other than Google. An unparalleled distribution channel with over 4.75 billion pieces of content shared every day, Facebook offers you one of the most powerful tools you can use to connect, engage, and build relationships with your audience online. Set up a Facebook Page (you'll find the "Magazine" option listed under the Entertainment category), which is public, viewable to all (whether registered on Facebook or not), and allows anyone to become a "fan" and receive the updates you post by simply "Liking" your Page. Make sure to add Facebook "Like" buttons to your website and any articles (or content) that you publish online.

Magazine Name	Facebook ID	No. of Likes
Cosmopolitan Magazine	Cosmopolitan	5,797,607
The Economist	TheEconomist	5,170,700
Newsweek	Newsweek	686,936
Reader's Digest	Readers Digest	2,379,995
Sneaker Freaker	snkrfrkrmag	970,987

Tip: With Facebook Pages, you can customize your URL with your magazine's name so that your address will read www.facebook.com/yourmagname. The only requirement is that you have more than twenty-five fans. To register your customized URL, go to: www.facebook.com/username.

TWITTER

Twitter (www.twitter.com) is a real-time microblogging platform where you broadcast short messages (called tweets) that consist of up to 140 characters in length. The network is based on the premise that you use your outgoing messages to answer the question of "What's happening?" But those 140 characters can be used for so much more. You can "retweet" (or repost) and share the content of others, receive private Direct Messages (DMs) from users who are following you and you are following back (that's the criteria), and use the @ sign to publicly start a conversation with, or reply to absolutely anybody who exists in Twitterland. For instance, I could send a tweet that reads "@magazinexyz enjoyed the article on The Top Ten Beauty Mistakes People Make that was published today, thanks," and you could reply with the following tweet: "@lorraine_phill glad you enjoyed it, look out for more next month." The hashtag (#) symbol allows you to categorize your tweets by keyword in a way that makes them searchable and findable on Twitter. For instance, if your area of expertise is social media marketing, you may want to end your tweets that are relevant to the subject with "#smm" so that people interested in the topic can easily find and follow you. On the other hand, you can use the hashtag symbol to perform a real-time search to find people who are currently having conversations or asking questions about your particular subject matter. This allows you to immediately connect with them and start a conversation right away. Visit Tagdef (www.tagdef.com) for a hashtag directory. If you've decided to use this network for your magazine, then don't forget to add Twitter "Follow" and "Tweet" buttons to your website and online articles.

Magazine Name	Twitter ID	No. of Followers
Entertainment Weekly	@EW	3.56 Million
InStyle	@InStyle	3.01 Million
People Magazine	@PeopleMag	6.15 Million
Time	@Time	7.18 Million
wired	@wired	4.3 Million

PINTEREST

Pinterest (www.pinterest.com) is a visual bookmarking site that allows you to "pin" images and videos to virtual pinboards that you categorize according to a subject or theme. Users have the ability to like, comment on, or have a conversation about a pin. People can follow you or your pinboards. They can "repin" your content onto their own boards, and you can in turn follow users or their boards and can repin their content onto your own boards. It is possible to create group boards that allow you to collaborate with others you decide to invite as contributors. According to social media analytics firm ZoomSphere, magazines are top performers on Pinterest, accounting for more than fifteen of the fifty most followed commercial entities currently appearing on the network. Because each pin added using the "Pin It" button links back to the website it was sourced from, Pinterest is known to be a wonderful website traffic generator. The only social networking site that currently drives more traffic than Pinterest is Facebook.

Magazine Name	Pinterest ID	No. of Pins	No. of Followers
Better Homes and Gardens	bhg	19,200	876,679
Elle	elle	40,897	270,935
Martha Stewart Living	ms_living	28,949	695,069
Real Simple	realsimple	16,097	574,065
Women's Health Magazine	womenshealthmag	5,845	317,955

INSTAGRAM

Instagram (www.instagram.com) is a social network and mobile app that allows users to take pictures and share them either on Instagram itself or on other popular networks such as Facebook and Twitter. When you launch the Instagram app from a mobile device it effectively takes the place of the default camera app and provides a bunch of fun filters that allow you to creatively change the appearance of a snap. According to statistics an average of 70 million photos are shared through the app each day and engagement on Instagram is 15 times that of Facebook. (Now that's something to think about!) Just like Twitter, you can use hashtags to categorize your magazine's content. For more options than are offered through the Instagram interface, you can use tools like Iconosquare (www.iconosquare.com) to better manage your community, administer photo contests, and track the performance of your magazine through the use of analytic tools.

Magazine Name	Instagram ID	No. of Photos	No. of Followers
GQ	gq	3,044	1.5 Million
Interview Magazine	interviewmag	2,496	332,000
Nylon Magazine	nylonmag	6,207	693,000
Paper Magazine	papermagazine	1,396	187,000
Teen Vogue	teenvogue	3,532	1 Million

GOOGLE+

Google+ (plus.google.com) presents another platform on which you can engage and interact with your audience online. Just like the other networks, you can post content updates of various kinds, and people who have selected to follow you will see them appear in their stream. They can either comment on, share, or "+1" a post (which is the equivalent of a Facebook "Like" and ultimately gives a stamp of approval). When you post content to Google+ (hashtags can also used on the network), it is immediately indexed by Google's search engine, which allows for greater exposure. Also, Google's personalized search function means that when you post content to Google+, that content is more likely to appear in your followers' search results for relevant searches that take place on Google's website. Google Hangouts allow magazines to reach out and connect with their audience through live, face-to-face video chats, and Google Communities allow you to further connect with and gain insight from readers by creating, joining, or participating in groups with those who share similar interests. If you are planning to use this network, make sure to add Google +1 buttons to both your website and online articles.

Magazine Name	Google+ ID	No. of Followers
Forbes	+Forbes	3,760,238
Glamour	+glamour	3,576,425
Martha Stewart	+MarthaStewart	2,431,760
The New Yorker	+newyorker	591,379
Sports Illustrated	+sportsillustrated	2,742,788

Tip: As you use the networks and start to share links, whether it's to your own content or the content of others, the services provided by Google URL Shortener (http://goo.gl) and bitly (http://bit.ly) allow you to shorten lengthy URLs, making it much easier for you to share, tweet, or email them out. Both services provide click statistics that allow you to easily measure the number of clicks your links receive.

PART III

Taking Care of Business

Chapter 15:
Monetizing Your Magazine

Magazine-a-nomics

I should imagine that as fun as magazine publishing is, you'd eventually like to see your publication turn a profit, maybe even to the point where you can finally quit that dreaded day job. But hold your horses, not so fast—there's a lot that has to happen before you can get to that point.

The first thing you'll need to do is figure out how much revenue your magazine needs to generate before you consider it as being profitable. The way to do that is by first estimating your costs. As the saying goes, "It takes money to make money," so you can expect to incur a bunch of expenses up-front. You should plan for these in advance so that you can safely keep yourself afloat before you begin to realize a return.

In the beginning, your costs will be divided into four sections: start-up costs, production costs, fixed costs, and variable costs. Your start-up costs will include everything you initially need to get your magazine off the ground. Items like the business license and registration fees, trademark registration, and any equipment or software you need to purchase to get your publication up and running would be considered a start-up cost.

Your production costs cover everything it takes to get your magazine produced. You will need to pay for content, artwork (photography and illustrations), layout and design, editing, proofing, models, location expenses, props—and the list goes on.

Fixed costs remain the same regardless of the level of sales or activity within the business. Examples include rent, post office box rental fees, bank fees, the internet connection charge, web hosting fees, and staff salaries.

Variable costs change in proportion to the level of sales or activity within the business. Examples include marketing and promotion activities, the cost of acquiring a commissioned salesperson (if you decide to go that route), and the fees associated-with hiring freelancers such as photographers, web designers, or programmers.

Figure 19 overleaf gives a list of costs you may need to incur to start your magazine. Depending on your frequency of publication, you may want to work out the costs for an entire year and then break it down from there so you can figure out the cost associated with producing each issue. It's literally unheard of that a magazine will come out of the gate generating a profit, as it will take time before you get into the groove editorially, spread the word, build a paid-subscriber list, or manage to garner the attention and trust of advertisers. But that is—of course—what you will be working towards all along.

Fill in the costs as best you can. Having read the previous chapters, you should have enough information to make reasonably accurate assumptions as to what you will need to get your project off the ground. When you arrive at a final amount, I suggest you add in at least 25 percent to allow for any unforeseen expenses or inflation price hikes—it's better to be safe than sorry. There are four main sources of income for a magazine:

1. Advertising revenue (print and digital)
2. New and renewal subscription revenue
3. Single-copy sales
4. Ancillary income

The secret to calculating a magazine's required profit level is to estimate the costs and then figure out exactly how many single copies and subscriptions you need to sell, how much you need to charge per ad, and how many ads you need to sell per issue to eventually become profitable.

Don't just skip over this section. Number crunching is never fun (and actually hated by most creatives) but it's better to have an idea now so that you can realistically plan your finances and estimate what you will need to keep your magazine going, rather than experience setbacks or surprises that can permanently put your magazine out of business later on down the line. You don't want to be that publication that launched one issue and was never heard of again so I advise that you kick back and get tucked in.

Most magazines start out containing little or no advertising, so it's expected that you won't be able to recoup all expenses and generate a profit from (at least) the first couple of issues, but as your magazine grows and advertising, subscription, or single-copy sales pick up, ideally you should be able to recoup expenses over time. Your main focus during this time should be to heavily market your publication, build relationships, create communities, and increase readership–those are the factors that will ultimately determine your success. Entice readers to become loyal subscribers by offering a free issue, a free trial, or even a free subscription. Do whatever you need to do to grow your readership level and lock your readers in for the long term.

About Advertising

According to The Association of Magazine Media magazine ads are an extremely powerful medium for increasing purchase intent and trumped as number one in both advertising attention and receptivity. Readers enjoy browsing through ads and consider them as an integral part of magazines. A reader's feelings of connection and trust for a particular publication often creates a halo effect, and this feeling of goodwill is extended to the advertisers presented. As a result, readers are more likely to take action

Figure 19 Start-up Costs Worksheet

Expense Type	Description	Amount ($)
Business	Business license and registration	
	Incorporation fee	
	Trademark registration	
	Banking fees	
	Rent/PO Box rental	
	Phone and fax line rental	
	Internet connection fee	
	Bipad/Bar code/UPC	
	Miscellaneous: Utilities, etc.	
Office Supplies	Pens, paper, stapler, envelopes, mailing labels, folders, printer ink, etc.	
Equipment	Computer/Laptop	
	Printer	
	Digital camera and memory card	
	External backup hard drive	
	Miscellaneous: discs, cables, batteries, equipment bags, etc.	
Website	Domain name registration	
	Hosting fees	
	Web designer/ Programmer/ Developer	
	Web maintenance fee	
	WordPress (or other) theme or software	
	WordPress additional costs (membership plug-in, etc.)	
	Website additional costs (shopping cart software, etc.)	
	Miscellaneous: Other website costs	
Software	Page layout and design software	
	Image editing software	
	Audio editing software	
	Video editing software	
	Microsoft Office (or equivalent)	
	Miscellaneous: Other software	

Design	Logo design	
	Business card layout and design	
	Media kit layout and design	
	Magazine layout and design	
	Subscriptions card layout and design	
	Promotional flyer layout and design	
Editorial (per issue)	Content	
	Artwork: Photographer(s)	
	Artwork: Stock photography	
	Artwork: Illustrator(s)	
	Miscellaneous: Editing, proofing, models, hair, makeup, etc.	
Production	Magazine print cost	
	Subscription card print cost	
	Business card print cost	
	Miscellaneous: Other production or print costs	
Distribution	Postage: Wholesalers	
	Postage: Subscribers	
	Postage: Single-copy	
	Postage: Other	
Marketing and promotion	Magazine mail out costs	
	Advertising costs	
	Miscellaneous: Other marketing costs	
Salary Expense	Staff salaries	
Professional Services	Consulting fees (Business consultant, lawyer, accountant, etc.)	
Miscellaneous Expenses	Electronic barcode creation (PIPS or other)	
	Business reply mail service permit fees (from USPS)	
	Membership/Association/Conference fees	
	Training	
	Other	
TOTAL COSTS		**$**

with regards to the product or service being offered—with statistics showing that a whopping 61 percent of magazine ads prompt readers to take some kind of action, whether that meant making a purchase or looking for more information. The same could not be said of both TV and radio ads.

Advertisers buy space in a magazine (or on a website) to target particular niche markets who may be interested in buying their products. To find advertisers for your publication, check the competition to see who currently and consistently advertises with them. Your media kit will present potential advertisers with all the information they need so they can make an informed decision. As you do not have a track record to justify your ad prices just yet, it is unlikely that you will be able to sell advertising to major companies in your first issue, so you must initially concentrate on generating single-copy and subscription sales (or other income generating schemes) in order to stay afloat. Major advertisers typically don't become interested until you reach around 10,000 plus in circulation—so it's safe to say forget about Coca-Cola and Clorox for now. Instead, approach small businesses, mom-and-pop stores, or websites that target your particular niche market.

Initially, it may be worth giving a few ads away for free in order to increase credibility in the eyes of your audience. The effort and cost of producing a print or digital ad may cause potential advertisers to shy away from a free offer, so consider providing design services at cost or for free as an added incentive. In addition, if you support a particular cause and would like to use a ready-made ad, free public service ads across various media are available for download from PSA Central (www.psacentral.org).

The Different Types of Advertising

There are numerous options available that you can use to monetize your magazine. Here are some of the most popular choices. When thinking about digital, remember not to compromise, cheapen, or clutter your site with too many annoying, obtrusive, distracting ads that take away from your content, which should always remain your primary focus. Without great content, you won't have readers, and without readers, you won't attract advertisers; so it's great content first and everything else after that.

In-page ads: Ads of specified sizes and dimensions that appear inside a magazine for a set fee.

Newsletter ads: Allows you to monetize your newsletter by offering space to advertisers that provides them with direct access to your highly targeted email subscriber list.

Classified ads: Low-priced small ads or announcements that usually appear at the back of a magazine.

Advertorials or sponsored content: Advertisements that appear in editorial form and give information about a product or service but are designed to look like objective journalistic articles. Most publishers feel that these types of ads should be clearly labeled "advertising feature" or "paid advertisement" so as not to confuse or "trick" a reader and compromise integrity.

Sponsorship: Allowing a company to pay to be the only advertiser that appears within an issue, or a set number of issues, in a magazine.

Paid content: Where you sell access to certain parts of your website

Google AdSense ads: A free, simple program that allows a publisher to earn money by displaying targeted Google text, image, video, or rich media ads on a website. Revenue is generated on a per-click (where an advertiser pays every time an ad is clicked) or per-impression (where an advertiser pays every time an ad is displayed regardless of whether it is clicked) basis.

Web banner ads: Ad images embedded into a web page that allow a visitor to click through to the associated site for more information. The advertiser pays the content provider somewhere around five to ten cents for every click the banner receives regardless of whether a purchase is made or not. Although this type of advertising is on the decline and not really conducive to mobile viewing, plenty of banner exchange programs are still available across the web.

Affiliate program ads: Where you partner with an online merchant to receive a referral fee or commission from the conversions that occur when a customer clicks on the affiliate's link or banner ad and performs a desired action such as making a purchase or signing up for a newsletter.

Setting Your Ad Rates

Most commercial print magazines set their ad rates using the CPM method (see page 36), and the same metric is currently used for digital also. To establish the average CPM for magazines that are comparable to yours, find their media kits online and study their rate sheets. You should aim to offer slightly lower prices in order to attract or steal (yes, it can be a dirty business) some of your competitors' advertisers away.

After you have set your basic rates, it will be necessary to adjust them for special instances such as early payment, frequency discounts, the particular dimension selected, small business or nonprofit charge, agency discounts, and a special position charge for ads that are placed in prime positions, such as the inside front cover, inside back cover, back outer cover, center spread, or within the first few pages of the magazine.

Once an ad has been sold and laid out as a spread in the magazine, always send a soft-copy proof (especially is you're designing it in-house) for sign-off and approval. It will be necessary for you to create an advertiser agreement to facilitate this process. Also, I recommend that you not include the ad in your final layout until payment has been received in full.

Selling The Ads

In the beginning it is likely that you are going to be selling most of the ads yourself. This is not a bad thing at all, as who knows your magazine better than you? Before making calls or sending out emails, learn as much as you can about your prospective advertiser to find out and reiterate the ways that your magazine can benefit them.

Aim to sell ads by annual contract, and offer the appropriate frequency discount. This way, you are not scrambling or desperate to find advertisers for every single issue. Although this does not mean you should ever stop your quest for advertisers, at least there will be pages you do not have to worry about either generating or creating in subsequent issues.

Know your media kit inside out so you are ready to answer any question an advertiser may have. Start with an introductory email that includes a mock version of your magazine and your media kit, or alternatively just cold call a prospect. Although it may be frightening at first, after a few calls you will become much more confident and relaxed. Start with the prospects you are least interested in acquiring and use these as warm-ups.

Think ahead and find any synergies you can exploit that may exist between the articles or particular themes that appear on your editorial calendar and the individual advertiser's products or services. Will you include a special advertiser page that appears within your magazine or on your website that showcases an advertiser's logo and provides a direct link to their site? Think of ways you can really add value and incorporate these ideas as a part of your enticing offer. Aim to create a win-win situation for both you and your potential advertiser.

Sound enthusiastic and excited about your magazine and about the potential partnership. Ask questions to get them talking. Listen carefully to their answers to find out more about their marketing needs in order to fit them to what your magazine has to offer. Let them know about the upcoming launch and the media coverage you will receive, which will be extended to their business.

Make sure to establish deadlines and specify what the next steps are. If the advertiser is local then you may want to pay them a visit making sure to bring along the mock version of your magazine and your media kit. Keep detailed notes of all your interactions whether by email, phone, or in person so you can remember everything that was discussed and the actions that will be necessary for follow-up.

If you just cannot fathom carrying out the sales aspect yourself, then think of other people who could possibly help out. Consider hiring a sales rep, freelancer, stay-at-home mom, retiree, friend, college student—the possibilities are endless. All you need is someone who is enthusiastic about your project and has a great telephone manner. Compensation offered for the sale of an ad can range from 15–20 percent.

Chapter 16:
Circulation and Distribution

Why Distribution

Finding readers for your publication will depend on various factors such as the subject matter, type of content, the particular market segment targeted, desired geographic reach (local, national, or international), the type of circulation model used (paid or unpaid), and your available budget. Once you have identified readers for your magazine, you will have to come up with creative ways to actually reach them, not forgetting, of course, to figure in the costs associated with each method.

According to statistics published by the Association of Magazine Media, subscription sales accounted for 92 percent of total circulation revenue, while single-copy sales accounted for 8 percent. Supermarkets accounted for 35 percent of all single-copy purchases, followed by supercenters (12 percent), drugstores (11 percent), bookstores (10 percent), and "other" locations (32 percent). The "other" category included outlets such as mass merchandisers, convenience stores, airport terminals, the newsstand, and discount stores.

How can you get your magazine into these locations and in front of prospective buyers? Through distribution—where the ultimate goal is to turn casual single-issue buyers into paid subscribers. It also makes your magazine look more credible in the eyes of a potential advertiser as it's quite impressive to say, "Yes, we're currently being carried by Barnes and Noble, so we're available nationwide."

What Distributors Do

A distributor acts as the intermediary between you (your publication) and the wholesalers, who distribute and deliver your magazine to specific territories and retail stores. The wholesaler is a vital link in the distribution chain, as their distribution expertise and network familiarity allows them to target the best regions and retail channels for your magazine according to your specific audience.

Distributors carry a catalog of titles that it offers for sale to various outlets. They make their money by taking a percentage of each issue sold. And are ultimately responsible for representing your magazine in the marketplace, performing duties such as marketing to wholesalers, taking orders, overseeing magazine deliveries, administering returns, and collecting all monies due.

So how much do they charge for these services? On average, about 55 percent of your cover price (which includes wholesaler and retailer charges), leaving you with 45 percent. Most publishers balk at the numbers when they first hear them, but can you figure out a cheaper, more efficient way to bring your magazine to the masses? This is your distributor's job, and it's one less rather difficult, time-consuming, logistics duty that you have to perform.

The average sell-through rate is less than 50 percent, so for every hundred magazines you send, you can expect to sell up to fifty of them. It's an expensive game and the unsold copies are either completely destroyed or the covers are ripped off and returned. In the case where the magazines are completely destroyed, you will receive what is called an "affidavit of returns," which is a statement that shows how many magazines did not sell. Most stores do not typically process returns until they receive your next issue.

Getting A Deal

LIST OF DISTRIBUTORS

Barnes & Noble Newsstand (http://bit.ly/bnnewsstand)
Comag (www.comag.co.uk)
Disticor (www.disticor.com)
Hudson News (www.hudsonnews.com)
Ingram (www.ingramcontent.com)
Kable Media Services (www.kable.com)
Kent News (www.kentnews.com)
The News Group or TNG (www.thenewsgroup.com)
Ubiquity (www.ubiquitymags.com)

Online newsstand services serving print magazines:
Mag Nation (www.magnation.com)
Newsstand (www.newsstand.co.uk)

Take a look at the distributor list above and visit their websites to find out what types of magazines they carry. You can also give them a call or send them an email to request a catalog of their titles. Find out if they distribute magazines that are either similar to yours or that target your desired readership.

After you have compiled a list of distributors who you feel may be a good fit, mail or email a copy of your magazine, your media kit, and an introductory letter (on company letterhead) to each one, making sure that your letter is addressed to the correct person and department. Positions in the magazine industry change frequently, so it is of the utmost importance to double-check all contacts before mailing anything out.

Your letter should be a one-page summary about your magazine. Pull the appropriate information from your media kit, including when you started, what your concept is, what your content consists of, why there's a need for your publication, and how you are different from others in the marketplace, as well as your frequency, page count, and selling price. Make your summary as professional and interesting as possible to encourage the recipient to actually take a flick through your magazine. Distributors look at your quality of content and design, the number of pages, and your advertising-to-editorial ratio. In general, they judge whether your magazine can stand up to—and compete with—other titles that are currently on the newsstand.

You will need to decide whether to send an actual copy of the magazine or just a dummy. A dummy is a mock version of your magazine that shows how the final piece will look. We sent out a dummy, but depending on the company you approach, some will request to see one or two copies of the actual publication. Check with distributors to find out what their preference is.

Our dummy consisted of the actual articles, graphics, and layout of the intended final piece. For advertisers, we included pages that said "Your Ad Here" to indicate the spaces that were available for ad placement and that we expected to fill. It was letter-sized at 8½ x 11, ninety-six pages long (with cover), saddle stitched and featured full color on both the interior and exterior pages. As we only needed a few copies made, we had them printed over at LuLu (www.lulu.com). I found the price there to be very affordable.

After performing a mail-out, give distributors at least two weeks before making follow-up calls. (In my case, I received a "majors" contractual offer

Figure 20: Example Letter to Distributor

April 15, 2017

Distribution Company
Address
City, State Zip

Dear <Contact Name>,
Per your request, please find enclosed a copy of SisterPower Magazine and accompanying media kit.

For the past eight years SisterPower.com has been the number one destination for African American women on the web. While the majority of publishers go from print to web, SisterPower launches with the advantage of already having a loyal audience who we thoroughly understand and are familiar with. With most of the editorial content being actually submitted by our readers themselves, this has enabled us to keep our finger on the pulse of our audience and deliver a magazine that is meaningful and relevant to them and their life experiences.

We are very excited to discuss distribution strategies with your company. The magazine plans to publish quarterly with a selling price of $6.95.

I will follow up with a call next week once you have had time to review the materials. Should you have any questions beforehand please do not hesitate to call, my cell number is (678) XXX-XXXX.

Thank you for your consideration,
Yours sincerely,

Lorraine Phillips
Publisher

PO Box 123456, Atlanta, GA 30036 • Phone:404.123.4567 • Fax:404.123.4567 • Email:sisterpower@sisterpower.com
W W W . S I S T E R P O W E R . C O M

in the mail, one "minors" offer by phone—which was later followed up by a contract in the mail—and a faxed order from a distributor, where no contract was necessary.) Ask if your magazine has been received and whether they would be interested in picking you up at this time.

In case of rejection, remain pleasant and thank the distributor for taking the time to look at your package. Respect their decision, as they are the experts in the field. Ask for constructive criticism and feedback on the areas where you need to improve. It's your first time in the game, so you are not going to know everything up front, and sometimes someone will point something out that, once said, seems so obvious to you.

Let them know that as your magazine continues to grow and evolve, you will be submitting more copies in the future. Keep in touch by sending them future issues. You never know, after they see improvements in your magazine, you may get picked up some time in the future. Now aren't you glad you remained courteous on the phone, even though you were highly disappointed at the time?

Your Contract

Not all distributors require a signed contract, but in cases where they do, your contract will be a negotiable agreement between you and a distribution company, granting them the right to distribute your magazine as best they see fit. Before signing a deal, get references from magazines they are currently working with, and give those publishers a call to ask questions about your potential distributor and how the deal is working out for them. The main points of your contract will include:

Contract time period and subsequent renewal terms
Contract terms may last for one year or more, depending on your frequency of publication.

Rights to distribute the publication

Some magazines may wish to use more than one distribution network, depending on the territories or stores served. Although this may not be necessary with some of the larger distributors, check whether your deal requires exclusivity. Look for a statement similar to "PUBLISHER hereby grants to the DISTRIBUTOR the sole and exclusive right to distribute the publication throughout the world." With my magazine, there were specialty bookstores and organizations that we wanted to personally distribute to, which was not a problem due to the provisions of our contract.

Distributor discount amount

Your distributor receives around 55 percent off the cover price, which means that if your magazine sells for $6.95, you will receive $3.13 of that, while your distributor receives $3.82. Once the appropriate costs are figured in, most small niche magazines often find the newsstand distribution model not to be worth their while, and some have even taken the view of newsstand distribution as being a necessary marketing expense.

When you can expect payment

Your contract will specify the exact number of days until you can expect payment, which is calculated from the off-sale date of each given issue. This will range anywhere from two to six months after your issue comes off the shelves. Remember, your distributor has to get paid before they can pay you.

How unsold magazine returns are processed

Instead of whole copy returns of a publication, you will receive either (a) the magazine covers or (b) an affidavit. In the case where you receive an affidavit, make sure you check the figures against your payment amount. In addition, your distribution company may reserve the right to destroy the magazine covers, so if you really want to see and count those covers for yourself, make sure to address this point in your contract.

The costs a publisher is responsible for

Although most contracts are pretty straightforward and easy to decipher, some may be loaded with frivolous hidden expenses. At a minimum, expect to be responsible for the cost of production, printing, and shipping expenses to wholesalers.

The reports and statements your distributor is responsible for

Verify what reports and statements your distributor is responsible for producing and within what time frame. Typical reports include sell-through information, accounting information, regional marketing data, allotment reports, and monthly sales statements.

Termination of contract

If things do not work out between you and your distributor and you decide to part ways for whatever reason, find out the necessary steps it will take to release yourself from the contract. In particular, find out what happens to monies due at the time of termination and whether you will be liable for any expenses.

After The Deal

You've signed the deal, so now what? Once signed, you will have to provide sample copies of your magazine—and any other promotional materials you may have—to your distributor so they can start marketing and promoting your publication. Some wholesalers like to see that you can consistently deliver at the same quality or better, and will wait for more than just one issue before they show an interest in your title. Exercise patience, don't get disappointed, and work hard on readying future issues.

If you do receive orders, your distributor will provide you with a shipping galley, which lists the wholesaler's name, address, and the number of magazines ordered. Most wholesalers will initially start with a small draw so they can test your magazine in the marketplace. Our orders ranged from fifty to three hundred copies per wholesaler.

You will be responsible for filling those orders and shipping the boxes directly to these wholesalers. If your printer does not provide shipping services, you can either arrange to pick them up and ship them yourself or use a business that specializes in mailing and distribution services. These types of companies plan and arrange cost-effective mailing strategies, oftentimes through shipment consolidation. Depending on the quantity to be shipped, this may turn out to be your preferred method.

Know that your distributor is hard at work marketing your magazine and the many other titles they carry. You can make sure you don't get lost in the mix by checking in every now and again to find out how marketing efforts are going, what the general consensus is out there, and whether there has been any progress with sales; or just to let them know how you are coming along with your next issue.

Your distributor is a newsstand specialist. I advise you to send them your completed magazine files (preferably in PDF format) for feedback and suggestions BEFORE going to print. It's a great precaution to take and may make the difference between receiving additional orders or not. Allot additional time into your production schedule for this task.

Unfortunately, distributors have a bad reputation for not paying on time, so you have to exercise due diligence when keeping track of money owed. Keep a list of the magazines shipped—to whom, on what date, the quantity, and any tracking information used for verification of delivery. Note your off-sale date for the issue and the date, according to your contract, when payment is due. When that date comes up, call or email your distributor to let them know you are expecting payment. Call every couple of weeks until your payment is received. Always be friendly and polite, as you don't want to tick anybody off, BUT remember, they are bound by contractual agreement to pay you.

Chapter 17:
Keeping It Legal

The Basics

To steer away from possible lawsuits, it is important to exercise sound judgment with your editorial decisions. Publishers and editors alike should acquire a basic understanding of the law as it applies to magazine publishing, with particular attention being paid to the following areas:

1. **Libel**

   Libel can be defined as "a published false statement that is damaging either to a person's reputation, a business, or a product." The key word in that sentence is *false*. This can mean inaccurate, untrue, or uncorroborated–the list goes on. All articles, references, headlines, photos, and illustrations should be examined thoroughly to diminish the likelihood of any legal liability.

2. **Invasion of privacy**

   People have the right to be left alone, have control of information published about them, and not be represented in a false light. Never obtain information using unscrupulous or questionable methods, and always require a signed agreement that gives consent and grants permission for you to publish a story, interview, graphic, or illustration.

3. Copyright infringement and plagiarism

Copyright infringement is the unauthorized use of a copyrighted work. There is a provision, however, called "fair use," which allows for the limited use of a copyrighted work without an author's permission. Unfortunately, there are no hard-and-fast rules for the definition of fair use, so I would advise you practice restraint in the use of others' materials. "Borrowing," or using a couple of words in the creation of a new work, is different from lifting or quoting several paragraphs of information. You can also run into the issue of plagiarism, which is using someone else's work or ideas without acknowledgment and then falsely claiming them to be your own.

Trademarking Your Magazine's Name and Logo

A trademark is a distinctive word, name, mark, emblem, or symbol that is legally registered to identify the goods made or sold by a person or entity and to distinguish them from the goods made or sold by another person or entity. Although it is not absolutely necessary to register your name and logo, it is wise to do so. That way you can lock down and protect your magazine's title, notify others of its use and existence, and prevent other entities from using any similar names or symbols in the marketplace.

Trademark filing fees start from $300 depending upon the type of application submitted, and you can file online at the United States Patent and Trademark Office (www.uspto.gov). Although the process is not that difficult, I recommend you consult with a professional for advice beforehand. If you decide to file online, you will receive an electronic receipt by email within twenty-four hours, that contains the serial number associated with your application. The entire process can take anywhere from thirteen to eighteen months to complete. While awaiting a definitive response, you can always use the serial number provided to check the status of your application online.

Copyright For Your Magazine

Although copyright actually exists from the moment your magazine is created, you can choose to copyright an issue (and any subsequent issues) to officially protect your rights to the contents of your magazine and make it easier to prove ownership in the future. You will need to use form SE, which allows registration of a single serial issue of a publication. Form SE should only be used for magazines that have already been published. If your magazine has not been published yet, then you need to file under the "Literary Work" option instead.

The fee for registering a copyright online is $35 and $45 if applying by mail. The process is reasonably straightforward, and there's a PowerPoint presentation that demonstrates everything you need to do in order to file. I recommend reviewing the tutorial before you file. If and when your copyright is approved, you can expect to receive a certificate of registration within eight months. For more information or to file online, visit The United States Copyright Office (www.copyright.gov).

Contracts and Agreements

You need to prepare contractual agreements for anyone who works on or submits material to your magazine, including advertisers, writers, photographers, models, designers, illustrators, or any other freelancer you may hire. An agreement is exactly that–it is a clear outline of the terms upon which two parties agree to work together. It protects you from any lawsuits that could arise for such claims as copyright infringement, libel, or invasion of privacy.

You should save your signed contractual agreements forever, even if your publication ceases to publish for some reason. Always keep a backup for proof of anything that may come up in the future. Although various contract examples can easily be found online, it is important that you consult with a lawyer for guidance on preparing the legal documents that will be necessary for your magazine.

Writer Agreements

In brief, your writer agreement grants you the right to print and publish a story. It outlines how much you will pay as well as your rights to revise and edit a story. It requires that the author warrant he or she is the sole, original creator of the work. More importantly, the author has to agree to hold you, the publisher, harmless against any claim, demand, suit, or proceeding that may be brought against you for any reason in regards to his or her work.

Illustrator Agreements

Your illustrator agreement, much like your writer agreement, grants you the right to print and publish an illustration. It outlines how much you will pay and requires that the illustrator warrants that to the best of his or her knowledge the concepts, ideas, copy sketches, artwork, electronic files, and other materials produced do not infringe on any copyright or personal or proprietorial rights of others. He or she has to agree to hold you, the publisher, harmless against any claim, demand, suit, or proceeding that may be brought against you for any reason in regards to their work and that the work is considered a work for hire, where all concepts, ideas, copy, sketches, artwork, electronic files, and other materials related to the particular project become the property of the publisher.

Photography Agreements

When you work with a professional photographer, the photographer owns the image. Even though the image would not have been created if it were not for your assignment and you may have paid for its production, he or she still owns all rights to the image. Photographers make their living by selling the use of their work, not just by creating it. A standard usage agreement gives you the exclusive rights to use the image for a specified, agreed upon period of time. When that period has expired, the image is released from the agreement, and the photographer may sell usage of the image as stock or sell it outright to a buyer, or you can renegotiate for more time. Any commercial photographer can supply you with a usage agreement, it is not a form that you have to create yourself.

Model Release Form

You should get a signed model release anytime your photo contains recognizable images of people. Publishing an identifiable photo of a person without a model release signed by that person can result in a civil liability for whoever publishes the photograph. A model release says the person being photographed has given consent to be photographed and grants his or her permission for the images to be used for the purposes outlined in the agreement.

Minor Release Form

Similar to a model release, a minor release form applies to a model under the age of 18, who is considered a minor, and requires the signature of a parent or legal guardian to give permission for the image to be used. It is a good idea to get both parents to sign if possible, as this reduces the risk that one parent will try to revoke the consent given by the other.

Chapter 18:
Your Business Plan

Why You Need One

Although business plan creation is beyond the scope of this book, I decided to provide you with a little information, as there are some fundamentals you should take into consideration as you make the important decisions about your magazine. There are numerous books that focus on writing a business plan in detail, and I suggest you invest in one. I cannot stress enough the importance of creating a plan, after all you wouldn't get on an airplane that didn't have a navigation system, and you don't want to do that with your magazine either.

Once you have completed the work from previous chapters, it should be just a matter of plugging the information in. Once again, for the creative types this chapter will be the least favorite, but, it is absolutely necessary. A business plan in essence is the blueprint for your business. It helps you to view your business objectively from all angles and forces you to look for and find information you may have inadvertently neglected otherwise. The good thing is that once it's done, IT'S DONE–and you only have to update various sections as necessary. Hopefully, your plan will show that you can publish profitably based on your projected cost and revenue assumptions. Although it can be quite intimidating to prepare a plan for business professionals, bank managers, and investors, I will say that you should make your plan simple, easy to read, and personal to you, because if *you* don't understand it then nobody else will.

> **NOTE:** A complete sample magazine business plan is available for download from: publishyourfirstmagazine.com

Example Business Plan Outline

Quite simply, your business plan should contain the following sections:

EXECUTIVE SUMMARY

A one-page summary that highlights the main points of your magazine business plan.

INTRODUCTION

Magazine concept
Briefly describe your focus, concept, reason for being, and the magazine's voice or personality.

Goals and objectives
What would you like your magazine to accomplish or achieve? Raise start-up capital? Nationwide distribution? 2,000 subscribers at the end of year one? List the goals for your magazine here.

Key success factors

Outline what needs to happen for your magazine to be a success. Create milestones that will help you monitor and determine your magazine's progress and growth.

COMPANY DESCRIPTION

Company ownership

Describe your business type (sole proprietorship, partnership, limited partnership, limited liability company, nonprofit, etc.) and name the founding members or managing partners.

Staff positions and departments

Describe the different departments, positions, and duties. Also, discuss any outsourced services or freelancers that you intend to use.

Company location and facilities

Describe your company location (even if virtual) and the basic equipment, or set up, you will use to facilitate company business.

EDITORIAL MISSION

Editorial philosophy

Provide detailed information on your magazine's concept and mission.

Editorial formula

Describe frequency, single-copy price, subscription price, total number of pages, advertising-to-editorial ratio, CPM, and any special content that you plan to include.

Example table of contents

What will your magazine feature? Provide a list of departments, columns, and possible features.

Magazine style or design

How exactly will your magazine look? Describe how you plan to visually present your magazine so that it might convey the right voice and personality to your intended audience.

MARKET ANALYSIS

Market segment profile

Who are your readers? What are their interests? Where are they located? What's the highest level of education? Average annual household income? Marital status? Describe your market, giving both demographic and psychographic information.

Advertising analysis

If using an advertising model for your business describe the types of advertisers who you think would be interested in advertising to your target market and why. If you plan to generate income from your digital properties describe your plan for that also.

Market growth and trends

Describe the current state of the industry. What changes or trends do you foresee? How will this be of advantage to you?

MAIN COMPETITORS

Competition

Know your competitors. Identify who they are, what they do, how they do it, and why you consider them to be your competition.

SWOT analysis (Strengths, Weaknesses, Opportunities, and Threats)

In reference to your competition and the market as a whole, describe your advantages (what you can do that is different or better, and how), disadvantages (areas you need to improve in or experts and advisors you may need to hire), opportunities (existing market conditions that will be helpful in achieving your goals and objectives), and threats (realistic external obstacles you may face that might prevent you from achieving your goals).

MARKETING, CIRCULATION, AND DISTRIBUTION

Marketing and promotions
Where and how do you plan on marketing your magazine? What promotional vehicles will you use to acquire readers? Consider the vehicles used by your competition to reach the market also.

Circulation and distribution
How do you plan on getting your magazine into the hands of your readers? What methods will you use and how often?

MANAGEMENT TEAM

Describe your team's background, experience, skills, strengths, and areas of expertise. Make them look good!

FINANCIAL SUMMARY

Start-up costs summary
List your start-up costs as calculated from the start-up costs worksheet on page 168.

Executive summary of profitability
Outline estimated costs, revenues, and profits.

And there you have it!

Appendix A:
Industry News and Resources

Ad Age (www.adage.com)
The leading global source of news, intelligence, and conversation for marketing and media communities.

Alliance for Audited Media (www.auditedmedia.com)
Formerly known as the Audit Bureau of Circulations, the AAM is about industry professionals bringing accountability and confidence to the new world of media.

American Society of Magazine Editors (www.magazine.org/asme)
Founded in 1963, ASME works to defend the First Amendment, protect editorial independence, and support the development of journalism. In addition, ASME sponsors the National Magazine Awards, the annual Best Cover Contest, and the Magazine Internship Program.

The Association of Magazine Media (www.magazine.org)
Formerly known as the Magazine Publishers of America (MPA), the association is a nonprofit authority resource that provides facts, data, and research on the magazine industry.

Coverjunkie (www.coverjunkie.com)
Coverjunkie is all about creativity and inspiration. The website highlights some of the most creative magazine cover designs from around the world.

FIPP (www.fipp.com)
Worldwide magazine media association.

Folio Magazine (www.foliomag.com)
Magazine publishing industry news and information resource.

LinkedIn Magazine Publishing Group (http://bit.ly/limaggroup)
Created for publishing professionals from all over the world, this LinkedIn group consists of over 52,000 members. You need to be a member of LinkedIn to join.

McPheters & Company (www.mcpheters.com)
McPheters & Company specializes in strategic planning and research for brands and companies in media-related fields, including media owners, advertisers, and ad agencies.

MinOnline (www.minonline.com)
Covering media, publishing, and magazine news, min is the industry's trusted source on the consumer and B2B magazine business.

Mr. Magazine (www.mrmagazine.com)
Website and blog of magazine industry expert Samir Husni.

Periodical and Book Association of America (PBAA) (www.pbaa.net)
A not-for-profit organization for publishers, distributors, wholesalers, retailers, consultants, and industry service providers.

Pew Research Center: Journalism and Media (www.journalism.org)
A nonpartisan "fact tank" that provides information on the issues, attitudes, and trends shaping America and the world. They conduct public opinion

polling, demographic research, media content analysis, and other data-driven social science research.

PricewaterhouseCoopers (PwC) (http://bit.ly/pwcmagpub)
Global entertainment and media marketing news, includes magazine publishing key insights report.

Professional Publishers Association (PPA) (www.ppa.co.uk)
The voice of professional publishers.

Publishing Executive (www.pubexec.com)
Provides vital information to publishing and production professionals on matters relating to printing, production, eMedia, and more.

The State of the News Media (www.stateofthemedia.org)
Annual report by the Pew Research Center's Journalism Project examining the landscape of American journalism.

Statista (www.statista.com/topics/1265/magazines)
Statistics and facts on the US magazine industry.

Appendix B:
Essential WordPress Plug-ins

Note: The following plug-ins are available for free except where indicated.

Security

Because of WordPress' popularity and widespread use, the software is prone to hacker attacks, which can do anything from taking your blog completely offline for good to redirecting your traffic to another website altogether. Always remember to use strong passwords for your admin panel that contain mixed-case letters, numbers, and symbols and are at least 10 characters in length. In addition, use the following plug-ins to help bulletproof your WordPress installation.

Akismet

Checks comments and filters out spam. Comes standard with all WordPress installations but it has to be set up and activated.

Bulletproof Security

Simple but robust surveillance plug-in that comes with a one-click setup method.

iThemes

Rated as a #1 WordPress security plug-in, iThemes gives you over thirty ways to secure and protect your WordPress site.

Sucuri

A trusted provider of website security, this plug-in offers real time alerts, website security scanner, and a malware removal service.

UpdraftPlus

Backup and restoration made easy. Complete backups (manual or scheduled) to S3, Dropbox, Google Drive, Rackspace, FTP, SFTP, email, and others.

Search Engine Optimization (SEO)

Help your blog rank higher in search results by using any of the following plug-ins. Most users either install the All in One SEO Pack along with Google XML Sitemaps or just use WordPress SEO by itself, which includes sitemap generation. Sitemaps provide crawlers with a hierarchical list of pages that appear on a website so they can be found more easily.

All in One SEO Pack

With over 13 million downloads to date, All in One SEO Pack automatically optimizes your blog for search engines with several easy-to-use functions.

Google XML Sitemaps

This plug-in generates an XML sitemap that enables search engines like Google, Bing, Yahoo!, and Ask.com to better index your site.

SEO Friendly Images

SEO plug-in that automatically updates all images with appropriate the ALT and TITLE attributes that will increase the chance of your image appearing as results in image search engines.

WordPress SEO by Yoast

Considered the most complete WordPress SEO plug-in today, its features include optimization of page content, image titles, and meta descriptions as well as XML sitemap generation.

Membership

The following plug-ins promise to have your membership site—where you sell access to certain parts of your website or share bonus materials and exclusive content with your subscribers—up and running in no time .

iThemes Membership

Allows for a WordPress membership site with content protection. Functions include the ability to sell paid (or free) membership access, protect content based on membership level, add multiple membership products, delay (drip) individual content items based on membership tier, and add members-only digital downloads. iThemes Membership is priced at $167 for use on up to two websites and $150 for use on an unlimited number of domains.

Magic Members

Magic Members includes unlimited membership levels and the ability to offer different membership access to different areas. Also, the download manager protects downloads from being accessed by unauthorized members. It features seamless integration with AWeber, GetResponse, Constant Contact, iContact, and MailChimp; and also integrates with numerous payment gateways: 1ShoppingCart, PayPal Standard, PayPal Website Payments Pro, PayPal Express Checkout,

CCBill, Authorize.net, ClickBank, and WorldPay. Magic Members is priced at $97 for use on a single domain, $197 for use on up to three domains, and $297 for use on an unlimited number of domains.

Restrict Content Pro

Complete membership and content manager that allows you to create an unlimited number of memberships levels, including free, trial, and premium. You can manage members and their subscriptions, track payments, offer discounts with a complete discount code system, and provide premium, members-only content to your subscribers. Restrict Content Pro is priced at $42 for use on a single domain, $86 for use on 2–5 sites, and $132 for use on an unlimited number of domains.

WishList Member

WishList lets you create free, trial, or paid membership levels; develop "modular" memberships with the ability to hide content from other levels; and automatically expire a membership after a certain time period. It integrates with PayPal, ClickBank, and other online payment solutions. WishList is priced at $97 for use on a single domain and $297 for use on an unlimited number of (personal) domains.

Social Media Sharing

Use any of the following plug-ins to make it quick and easy for readers to share content with their social networks.

Digg Digg

This floating share bar has a ton of customizable options and lets your audience share with popular networks such as Facebook (also includes the Facebook "Like" button), Twitter, Pinterest, Digg, LinkedIn, Google +1, reddit, Yahoo!, StumbleUpon, Delicious, and others.

Easy Social Share Button for WordPress

Supports twenty social networks, has twelve native social like, follow and subscribe buttons, includes a social fans counter, and comes with twelve built-in templates.

Shareaholic

Eye-catching floating and non-floating social sharing buttons that also has a related posts feature built right in.

ShareThis

ShareThis is a fully customizable share bar that allows for access to up to 120 social media channels. It includes email sharing capability and provides real-time analytics in the form of detailed reports—letting you track your most popular content and providing insight into social sharing behavior.

Related Posts

These plug-ins help to make your blog site "sticky" by listing related content that visitors can read or view.

nrelate Related Content

This plug-in uses patent-pending technology to continuously analyze a blog site's content and display other related content that appears on the site. You can easily customize the look of this plug-in by using one of the included set styles, or you have the option to design your own.

Yet Another Related Posts Plug-in (YARPP)

YARPP gives a list of posts or pages related to the current entry thereby introducing the reader to other relevant content on your site. It includes thumbnail support.

Miscellaneous

Broken Link Checker
The plug-in checks your posts, comments, and other content for broken links and missing images, and sends out a notification either via the dashboard or by email.

Contact Form 7
Simple and flexible contact form plug-in.

Disqus Comment System
Disqus replaces your WordPress comment system with a tool that makes commenting and participating in discussions much easier and more interactive for your readers. It allows visitors to conveniently use their Facebook or Twitter accounts in order to leave comments on your blog.

Google Analytics by Yoast
Allows you to easily track the activity on your blog and stays up to date with all the latest features in Google Analytics.

Jetpack by WordPress.com
This heavy-weight WordPress plug-in provides a multitude of functions, including email subscriptions to blog posts and comments; automatic posting to social networks such as Twitter, Facebook, Tumblr, and LinkedIn; a recent tweets widget; and an artificial intelligence-based spelling, style, and grammar check tool.

MailChimp for WordPress
Allows you to easily add MailChimp sign-up forms and sign-up checkboxes to your WordPress site. There's also a Pro version available that starts at $49 for a single site.

NextGEN Gallery

NextGEN Gallery does just about everything you'd ever want to do with images over and above the basics that are offered by WordPress.

TinyMCE Advanced

An advanced visual editor for WordPress that adds many features to the standard default editor, including the ability to compose a blog post in MS-Word and then copy and paste it directly into WordPress. Doing it without using this plug-in can cause problems as Word adds in hidden code that can oftentimes mess up the format of a WordPress post.

WooCommerce

Transforms your WordPress site into a powerful and extendable eCommerce store.

WPTouch Mobile Plug-in

WPTouch automatically transforms your WordPress website into a mobile-friendly version for tablets and smartphones. There's also a Pro version available that comes with over two hundred more features than the free version and is priced at $59 for a single domain license.

Glossary

Ad sales rep: Person responsible for calling and setting up appointments with advertisers; in charge of maintaining current accounts and generating new business.

Advertising director: Manages a staff of ad sales representatives; responsible for generating advertising in magazine through direct selling and promotional activities.

Affidavit of returns: A statement of returns that shows how many copies of a magazine were not sold through a particular distribution outlet.

Agreement: A negotiated and legally binding arrangement or document between two parties.

Alignment: The position of text on a page; can be left, right, centered, or justified.

Allotment: The number of magazines a publisher sends to a distributor, wholesaler, or retailer.

Alt attribute: The text description of an image that is displayed when a mouse hovers over the image on the web.

Ancillary products: A product or service a publisher can sell in addition to the magazine to extend their brand and generate additional income. Examples include hats, pens, bags, T-shirts, seminars, audio books, and other promotional items.

Aqueous coating: A clear, shiny, water-based coating which is applied like ink by a printing press.

Art director: Oversees the artistic design of the magazine and works closely with the editorial director to ensure that the design is consistent with the editorial philosophy.

Article: A piece of writing included in a magazine.

Artwork: Visual materials such as photographs or illustrations.

Associate editor: A staff editorial person who supports and assists the editor with writing, editing, and assigning material as required. May also be responsible for writing titles, subtitles, and captions.

Audit bureau: An organization that audits and verifies publishers' claimed circulation numbers. Advertisers then use these official reports. Reputable auditing companies include BPA Worldwide and the Audit Bureau of Circulations (ABC).

Authority site: A popular site that is frequently visited, contains large amounts of strong content, has numerous incoming links based on merit and relevance, and is often referred to as a trusted source. Amazon.com, Wikipedia.com, and YouTube.com are all examples of authority sites.

Autoresponder: Computer software or configuration that automatically responds to an incoming email.

Backlinks: Incoming links to a website or web page.

Bar code: Also known as a Universal Product Code, or UPC. It is a unique fourteen-digit number that allows retailers to track the sales of a magazine through computerized inventory control systems; provides information such as the magazine name, issue number, price, inventory available, and date the magazine should be removed from the racks.

Binding: A method of attaching pages together in a magazine; can be either saddle-stitched or perfect bound.

Bipad: The five-digit number contained in a magazine's barcode that uniquely identifies the magazine's title for the life of the magazine.

Bitmap images: Images that are created using a grid of individual pixels that are each assigned a different color or shade. Example formats include bmp, tiff, gif, and jpeg files.

Black hat SEO: Unethical and unacceptable search engine optimization practices that are not approved of by search engine companies.

Blacklist: A database of internet addresses, or IPs, known to be used by spammers and denied a particular privilege, service, access, or recognition.

Bleed: Artwork or color that extends off the edge of the page after trimming.

Blog: An interactive website on which an individual or a group of users publish thoughts; share views, ideas, and opinions; discuss issues; divulge information; give advice; report on breaking news; provide useful links, photos, and videos; or share expertise and knowledge.

Blogger: A person who writes, publishes, and updates a blog.

Blogging: The act of writing, publishing, and updating a blog.

Blogroll: A list of blogs recommended by a blogger, which can appear as a sidebar menu on a blog site. **Blow-in:** Method of inserting unattached cards between the pages of a magazine.

Body copy: The main text of a story.

Body type: The font used for body copy.

Book: Term used to describe a magazine.

Brand: The specific and unique identity of a business, product, or service.

Browser incompatibility: When a website displays incorrectly depending on the browser, browser version, platform, or device it is being viewed on.

Business manager: Supervises internal office management.

Business reply mail (BRM) service: A direct response vehicle that is used by businesses, publishers, government departments, and other organizations to seek responses from recipients within the US (Domestic Business Reply Mail) and from recipients around the world (International Business Reply Mail).

Byline: A particular author's name and brief biographical information that accompanies an article.

Callout: Text from an article that visually breaks up a page and draws a readers' attention.

Caption: Text that identifies a picture or image.

Center alignment: Where text is centered on a page leaving the same sized margin on either sides.

Circulation: The number of readers a particular publication has, calculated through the sum of single-copy and subscription sales.

CMYK (4 color, four color, full color, or process color): The four ink colors used for magazine printing: cyan (blue), magenta (red), yellow, and black. The four inks are combined in different quantities to reproduce and print (almost) all colors.

Coated paper: Chemically treated paper that has a glossy, shiny look to it.

Collate: To organize a set of individual sheets or signatures into the proper sequence for binding.

Color correct: To adjust the processed colors in order to achieve the desired results.

Column: Usually written by an expert, famous, or respected individual. A column provides credibility for the magazine and is usually written by the same person every month.

Consumer magazine: General or special interest magazine that is marketed to the public, usually available via newsstand or subscription, and more often than not contains advertising. The main purpose of these types of magazines is to entertain, sell products, and promote viewpoints. Examples include *Readers Digest* and *O Magazine*.

Content management system (CMS): Computer software or system used for organizing, managing, storing, and facilitating the creation of documents and other digital assets. Content management systems can either be online or offline.

Contributing editors: Writers who are experts in the field that the magazine covers. Regular freelance writers with whom the magazine wishes to maintain a relationship may also be given this title.

Conversion rate: The rate at which a casual visitor to a website is either converted into a customer or takes some type of desired action such as make a purchase, sign up for a newsletter, subscribe to an RSS feed, or download a file.

Conversion: A conversion is defined as the number of visitors who complete a desired action beyond just surfing and perusing a website.

Copy editor: Copy editors are not proofreaders. They check written material in its original form (before layout and design), looking for and correcting errors in grammar, spelling, usage, and style. They also check articles for form, length, and completeness.

Copyright infringement: The unauthorized use of a copyrighted work, in whole or in part, without the copyright owner's permission.

Copyright: Protects original works of authorship from use without permission.

Cost per thousand readers (CPM): The measurement of how much money it costs an advertiser to reach 1,000 readers. This amount is calculated by dividing the page price by the number of copies in circulation. If you have 5,000 readers and charge $1,000 per page, then the CPM = $1,000/5 = $200.

Cover line: The short title or teaser that appears on the cover of a magazine.

Crawler: An automated software program that scans the web with the purpose of storing and indexing web page information for search results.

Crop marks: Printed lines that show where a printed sheet should be trimmed.

Cropping: Cutting away parts of an image that are not required.

CSS (cascading style sheets): A style language that defines the format and layout of an HTML document.

Defamation of character: Can include libel, slander, or both.

Demographics: Statistical data relating to a particular group within the population, can include information such as age, income, and education level.

Department: The part of the magazine that a reader becomes familiar with and expects to see in every issue; offers consistency and establishes the tone and voice of your publication. A different contributor may write a department every month. They are grouped together under one common topic so an individual department may have one or several articles.

Design: The art of visual communication; utilizing color, type, illustration, photography, and layout techniques to present content or information that communicates effectively and is aesthetically pleasing to the eye.

Digital magazine: A highly interactive digital interpretation of a print magazine that can be read on an electronic device.

Distributor: A company that represents and sells a catalog of magazine titles to various retail outlets.

Draw: See *Allotment*.

Dummy: Mock version of the magazine that demonstrates how the final printed piece will look.

Edit: To modify or correct an article.

Editorial assistant: An entry-level employee who supports the more senior editors by performing duties such as researching information, setting up interviews, returning calls, making copies, and filing.

Editorial calendar: A schedule of upcoming editorial content to be featured in upcoming issues. It is used by advertisers to determine what issues may offer product tie-ins according to the planned theme and content.

Editorial director: Person responsible for all final editorial decisions and for managing and coordinating the creative staff to ensure that the publication's editorial philosophy is executed and fulfilled with each issue.

Editorial formula: Describes the actual make-up of the magazine, answering questions like: What is the frequency of the publication? Price? Subscription price? Number of pages? Advertising-to-editorial ratio? Number of columns? Number of departments? Number of features? Etc.

Editorial philosophy: Describes the magazine's main focus and reason for being.

Executive editor: Reports directly to the editor in chief; performs both managerial and editorial duties, keeping the magazine on schedule by enforcing strict deadlines.

Exit page: The last page visited by a reader before leaving a website.

Fact checker: Researches submitted articles and checks that the information presented is accurate.

Fair use: Allows for the limited use of copyrighted material without the need for the author's permission or attribution.

Feature: These are the longer articles in a magazine, usually four to six pages in length. They are unique to each issue and most clearly exhibit the magazine's concept.

Finish: The surface appearance of paper, examples include matte and gloss.

First serial rights: Grants the publisher the right to print an article for the first time before anyone else, but all other rights are retained by the author.

Flatplan: Used to plan and organize the layout and order of pages for publications such as magazines, newspapers, catalogues, and books. Flat plans originally started as drawn out pieces of paper that were stuck to a wall to show the order of articles and advertisements in a publication. As pages were moved or ads were cancelled, the pieces of paper could easily be moved around, annotated, or amended. Paper flatplans are being replaced by digital flatplans, many of which are able to sync with applications such as Adobe InDesign.

Font: A particular typeface, including upper and lower case letters, numbers, punctuation, and special characters.

Four color: See *CMYK.*

Freelancer: Person who sells or contracts their work to many different clients rather than actually being employed by one particular company.

Frequency: The number of times a year a magazine is published.

Frequency discount: A reduced advertising rate based upon the number of times an ad is placed in a magazine within a specified period of time.

Google Analytics: A free web analytics solution created by Google that gives insight into website traffic, performance, and marketing effectiveness.

Graphic designer: Responsible for how the magazine looks. A designer utilizes color, type, illustration, photography, and various print and layout techniques to create a design that effectively communicates and appeals to its intended audience.

Gutter: The white space formed by the two inner margins of the facing pages in a magazine.

Hashtag: Used as a special symbol on various social media sites to mark a specific keyword or topic in a way that makes it easy for people to find or follow a "conversation" on that topic.

Headline: An article's title, which acts as the attention-grabber for a story.

House sheets: Paper that is kept in stock by a printer and is therefore usually cheaper to print on.

HTML (hypertext markup language): A computer programming language designed and used to create web pages.

HTML5: Latest version of HTML that moves away from previous limitations and allows for much more dynamic functionality such as embedding audio and video, and displaying animations without the need for external plug-ins such as Adobe Flash (which is now considered outdated).

Illustration: A drawing or sketch.

Inbound links: Incoming links to a website or web page.

Indexing: A data structure that allows information to be conveniently indexed to a database schema for efficient retrieval.

Insert: A piece that is prepared for insertion into a magazine such as a subscriptions card.

International Standard Serial Number (ISSN): A unique eight-digit number assigned to a serial publication that is necessary when working with or selling subscriptions to libraries. The number uniquely identifies the title regardless of language or country where it is published.

JavaScript: A simple programming language often used in conjunction with HTML, or other web programming languages, in order to make web pages more interactive.

Justification: Positioning of text so that both the left and right margins appear in a straight line down the sides of a page.

Kerning: Adjusting the space between pairs of letters for a better fit.

Keyword prominence: The location or placement of a keyword in the source code of a web document. The higher up on the page or tag a keyword is, the more weight it is given by a search engine.

Keyword proximity: The closeness between two or more keywords.

Keyword research tool: A tool that helps select the most appropriate and effective keywords for a website.

Keyword rich: When a web page is full of relevant keywords.

Keyword stuffing or spamming: The process of adding a superfluous amount of keywords to a web page in such a way that the information ends up being nonsensical and user-unfriendly.

Keyword term or phrase: The specific term or phrase entered into a search engine by a user to search for information online.

Kill fee: The amount paid when a writer has been contracted to write an article but the article is never published.

Lacquer: Clear, shiny coating that is applied to a printed piece for protection.

Landing pages: A report that shows the most popular pages upon which visitors entered a site.

Layout: The way in which text and pictures are arranged on a page.

Leading: The space between the lines of type on a printed page.

Left alignment: Where text along the left margin appears in a straight line down the page, but the right margin is ragged or misaligned.

Libel: A published false statement that is damaging to a person's reputation, a business, or a product.

Logo: A distinguishing mark, emblem, or symbol that is used to identify a particular organization.

Long tail keywords: Keyword phrases of three words or more that allow for a narrow and distinct search for information online.

Margin: The edge or border of a page.

Marketing director: Individual responsible for the publicity and promotion of a magazine.

Media kit: Magazine promotional tool consisting of information on a magazine and usually includes the audience demographics, psychographics, market analysis, circulation numbers, editorial calendar, and advertising rates.

Microblog: A simple internet technology that allows a user to post short statements or sentences. Twitter (www.twitter.com) is an example of a microblogging service.

Mission statement: Statement that explains a company's aims, values, and reason for being.

Mockup: See *Dummy*.

Multimedia: Multiple forms of media, such as text, graphics, and sound, that are integrated together in some form.

Native file: The default file format which works with an application during the creation, edition, or publication of a file. For instance, a Microsoft Excel's .xlsx file is native to Microsoft Excel.

News aggregator: A website or computer software that aggregates a specific type of information or news from multiple online sources.

Newsletter: A periodic publication distributed digitally via email to an opt-in list of subscribers.

Niche market: A narrowly defined group of potential customers for a magazine's particular subject matter.

One-time rights: When the publisher can publish the article one time, but the writer retains the right to simultaneously sell it elsewhere.

Online community: A virtual community that consists of people who share common interests and use the internet (websites, forums, chat rooms, email, etc.) to communicate, exchange, or collaborate online.

Orphan: Undesirable text formatting where a word or a short sentence appears by itself at either the end of a paragraph, a column, or the bottom of a page.

Other magazines: Magazines that cannot be defined as either consumer or trade.

Outbound links: Links within a website that point to an external source.

Overrun: The number of magazines printed in excess of the quantity ordered.

Page count: The total number of pages in a magazine.

Page views: A statistic that shows the most popular pages that have been viewed on a website.

Pagination: The process of arranging the sequence of numbers assigned to the pages in a periodical.

Perfect bound: Book binding method where printed pages are shaved along the side and glued at the spine.

Perforate: To pierce or make holes in a printed piece.

Periodical: A publication that is published at regular intervals.

Photo editor: Person responsible for the visuals and images for a magazine's stories. This person can also be tasked with maintaining, cataloging, and storing images.

Plagiarism: Using someone else's work or ideas without acknowledgement and falsely claiming authorship of those works.

Plus cover: A cover that is on a different paper than the inside. In this case, the printing process for the cover would be different from the printing process for the pages that appear on the inside.

Podcast: A pre-recorded audio or video file that can either be streamed or made available for download online, and listened to or viewed on a personal computer or mobile device.

Point size: The unit of measurement used to describe the size of type and leading. There are seventy-two points in an inch.

Preflight: A software feature that helps package all the elements that a printer needs so the files can be accurately reproduced; includes fonts, pictures, and illustrations.

Premium position: Prime advertising position within a magazine that is sold at a higher rate. Positions include the inside front cover, inside back cover, back outer cover, or center spread.

Prepress: The process of getting a document ready for print.

Press release: A public announcement prepared for distribution to various news media outlets.

Printer: Vendor responsible for manufacturing the final product, printing, and binding the magazine.

Process color: See *CMYK*.

Production director: Creates, coordinates, and oversees the production schedule to ensure the magazine is produced on time. Can help staff members format material so all pages are complete and technically accurate. May also oversee the magazine's press run.

Production schedule: A plan or timetable that describes the workflow, tasks, and deadlines necessary to ensure that a magazine is produced on time.

Promotions director: See *Marketing director*.

Proof: A copy of the actual magazine that is used to check for errors and flaws in order to make corrections before the final piece is printed.

Proofreader: Checks over the final proof for typographical and mechanical errors.

Psychographic information: The study and classification of people according to their attitudes, aspirations, values, beliefs, and other psychological criteria.

Public relations (PR): Activities undertaken by a company or individual to protect, enhance, or build their reputation through the use of various media outlets and mediums.

Publication: A book, magazine, newspaper, journal, or musical piece that is offered for sale.

Publisher: Oversees the business side of the magazine and is ultimately responsible for the magazine's profitability. Duties include budgeting, strategic planning, and ad development.

Pull quote: A quote—usually not more than a sentence or two—that is extracted from the main text of an article and set off from other information on the page using lines, shading, or boxes.

Query letter: Introductory letter to an editor that describes the idea for an article that an author would like to submit.

Rate sheet: Summarizes a publisher's prices for ads of different sizes, colors, and positions. Also summarizes the frequency discounts for consecutive ads being placed in the magazine.

Resolution: Indicates the number of dots per inch and refers to the sharpness of an image.

RGB: The primary additive colors of red, green, and blue. When these colors are combined equally, they produce white, and when they are combined in different amounts, they can produce a broad array of colors. TV and computer monitors produce images using the RGB method.

Right alignment: Where text along the right margin appears in a straight line down the page, but the left margin is ragged or misaligned.

Rights-managed stock photography: A photo (or illustration) that is licensed for one-time, specific use only.

Robot: Software that scans the web with the purpose of indexing pages for search results.

Royalty-free stock photography: Allows for the unlimited use of a photo (or illustration) in any media as defined by the licensing agreement.

RSS (Really Simple Syndication or Rich Site Summary): Allows for the syndication or distribution of content, or a summary of content, to subscribers who are automatically notified every time new content is added to either a blog, website, or podcast series. The information is displayed through an RSS reader or news aggregator.

Saddle stitch: Book binding method where magazine leaves are secured through the centerfold by wire staples.

Sans serif: Fonts that are straight and have no serifs or curlicues at the end of the letters—generally used for headlines, sub-heads, and sidebars.

Scaling: Enlarging or reducing the size of an image.

Score: To crease paper along a straight line so it can be folded accurately.

Search engine optimization (SEO): The process of improving the visibility of a website or web page in a search engines' natural or unpaid organic search results.

Search engine rankings: The position of a web page returned in search results when searched for with a specific keyword or keyword phrase.

Search engine-friendly: Coding a web page in a way that makes it easily accessible and understandable to search engine spiders.

Search engine: A tool on the internet that is used to search for and display relevant information.

Second serial (reprint) rights: A nonexclusive license that gives the publication the right to publish a story, article, or poem after another periodical has already published the piece.

Self-cover: A magazine cover that is printed on the same paper stock as found on the inside.

Sell-through rate: The percentage of magazines sent to a distributor that is actually sold.

Senior editor: Writes, edits, proofreads, and copy-edits articles; helps assign articles to writers, making sure they understand the specifics. Other names for this title include feature editor, beauty editor, and so forth.

Serif: Fonts that have curlicues at the end of the letters, which make them easier to read. Serif fonts are generally used for body text.

Sheet-fed press: A printing press that prints on individual sheets of paper as opposed to rolls. This method is much slower and more expensive than using a web press.

Shipping galley: A list that a distributor provides that shows the name, address, and the number of magazines ordered by a wholesaler or retailer.

Short tail keywords: A one- or two-word search term, like the term "digital camera," that has a high search volume and is not very specific.

Sidebar: A short piece of text placed alongside a main article that is typically boxed off and contains additional or explanatory information.

Signature: A printed sheet that has been folded at least once and will become part of a magazine.

Single-copy sales: Magazines that are sold through a website, retail outlet, or an event.

Slander: A false spoken statement that is damaging to a person's reputation, a business, or a product.

Social media marketing: The process of gaining traffic or attention through the use of social media.

Social media: An interactive website that functions as a virtual community and allows a user to set up a profile and create, share, and exchange information or ideas with others online.

Spider: An automated software program that scans the web with the purpose of storing and indexing web pages for search results.

Spot color: A specially mixed ink that is applied individually on the printing press as opposed to a mix of the four (CMYK) inks which make up process printing. The most popular company that makes spot colors is Pantone, Inc. They sell color guides (or swatch books) that enable printers to mix and create the exact same colors from a set of base inks.

Spread: Two facing pages with an even-numbered page on the left and an odd-numbered page on the right.

Staff writer: Resident staff member who writes and contributes articles to the magazine.

Stock photography: Ready-made images available for download online.

Style guide: A written set of standards or rules that should be followed when either writing or designing documents for a specific publication, organization, or field.

Subscriptions card: The mail piece that appears inside a magazine that makes it easy for readers to subscribe.

Target market: A specific group of customers or a particular market segment that a product or service is marketed to.

Tracking: The process of adjusting the amount of space between the words on a page.

Trade magazines: Trade magazines are business-to-business magazines. Their audience consists of readers in a particular trade or profession.

Although some may be available on newsstands (e.g., *ComputerUser*, *Communication Arts*, etc.), most are sold through subscription only. Examples include *AJN: American Journal of Nursing* and *Cognitive Psychology*.

Trademark: A distinctive word, name, mark, emblem, or symbol that is legally registered to identify the goods made or sold by a person or entity, and differentiates them from the goods made or sold by another person or entity. Trademarks grant exclusive rights to the owner that prevent competitors from using similar marks in the marketplace.

Trim size: The final page size or dimensions of a magazine after it has been trimmed.

Typeface: See *Font*.

Typography: The art of setting and arranging type on a page.

Uncoated paper: Untreated paper.

Underrun: The number of printed magazines delivered that is less than the quantity ordered.

Unique visitors: Statistic that shows how many different people visit a website within a fixed time frame.

URL (Uniform Resource Locator): The address of a web page on the web.

UV coating: A high gloss, heavy coating that is applied to a printed piece or magazine cover. It is more expensive and durable than varnish coating.

Varnish: Clear, shiny coating that is applied to a printed piece for protection. Varnish is not as heavy or shiny as UV coating but is a cheaper alternative.

Vector graphic: A type of computer graphic created using mathematical formulas that can be enlarged or reduced without any loss of quality.

Viral marketing tools: Tools that make it easy for a visitor to share information about a site, company, product, or event etc. (also known as "word-of-mouth marketing").

Visit duration: Web statistic that shows how long visitors spend on a site (in increments of seconds) and how many pages were viewed within that time.

Web designer: Responsible for the creation, design, layout, and coding of a web page.

Web host: A service or company that allows individuals and organizations to display websites that can be accessed over the internet. Web hosts store HTML pages (and other types of code) on their servers.

Web press: A printing press that prints both sides simultaneously on large, continuous rolls of paper that are then cut into sheets after printing.

Web statistics: Tracks the number of visitors to a website and analyzes behavior, providing information on where visitors came from, what day and time they visited, how long they spent, what path they took, and other statistical information.

Website compatibility: Ensuring that a website displays and acts the same regardless of what browser, browser version, platform, or device it is being viewed on.

Website editor: Responsible for creating and editing web content.

Wholesalers: Companies that work on behalf of publishers to distribute and deliver magazine titles to specific territories and retail stores.

Widow: Undesirable text formatting where a paragraph ending line appears by itself at the top of the following page (or column) and is therefore separated from the rest of the text.

Word spacing: The amount of space between words.

WordPress: A web-based, open-source content management system (CMS) or blogging platform.

Work for hire: Where a copyright is transferred from an employee to the employer that the work was originally created for.

Writer's guidelines: Document created by a magazine for potential or interested contributors that describes exactly what the publisher is looking for in articles in order for them to be considered for publication.

About the Author

Lorraine Phillips attended Jackson State University, where she received an MBA in business administration and a BS in computer science, graduating both programs with honors and distinction. She later went on to earn an AA in graphic design from Bauder College and was elected to Who's Who Among Students in American Universities & Colleges for outstanding merit and accomplishments.

Lorraine, former publisher of *SisterPower Magazine*, is a creative information technology professional with over fourteen years' experience in planning, developing, and publishing print, internet, and digital projects. As an author Lorraine has received several awards where her books have been recognized for exhibiting superior levels of creativity and originality as well as high standards of design and production quality. She was also selected for what is one of the country's most respected book awards, being named a Benjamin Franklin Awards silver finalist in the Business and Economics category for excellence in book editorial and design.

Lorraine is currently a freelance user experience designer. As a dynamic speaker, author, freelancer, and coach, it is her mission to help people achieve their personal and professional dreams. As she puts it in her own words, "It's exactly what I was born to do!"

So I Published A Magazine

If you've ever thought about publishing a magazine and wondered what it would take, award-winning author Lorraine Phillips' latest release, *So I Published A Magazine* features sixteen honest, candid conversations with independent publishers from around the globe in order to find out exactly what it takes to start and run a magazine from the ground up.

Lorraine asked these publishers questions like: How did you initially fund your magazine? Did you do any market research or create a business plan prior to launching? How do you attract readers? What do you do to attract advertisers? How important is social media to your operation? Who handles distribution? What factors do you think contribute to the success or failure of a magazine? And much more.

Together, these publishers will help you create the blueprint for your very own publication. Featured magazines include: *Blow, Cereal, Concrete Wave, Delayed Gratification, Disegno, HOLO, IdN, Katachi, Lionheart, Little White Lies, PAPER, Sneaker Freaker, Things & Ink, 3x3, Very Nearly Almost (VNA),* and *Wax Poetics.*

So I Published A Magazine: Conversations with Independent Publishers from Around the Globe (ISBN: 9780988953536) is available from major book wholesalers, retailers, and various online outlets. For more information, please visit: soipublishedamag.com.

Publish Your First Digital Magazine, is a must-read for all creatives who are passionate about sharing a message with their audience and looking for innovative ideas, strategies, tools, and techniques they can use to create and distribute a digital publication.

With the digital magazine landscape being so new, the book covers much needed information on topics such as: magazine business fundamentals, how to create an editorial philosophy, how to build an editorial calendar, the different ways a digital magazine can be monetized, and the tools that will be necessary for producing a digital publication.

Publish Your First Digital Magazine: Taking You from Concept to Delivery, (ISBN: 9780988953505) is available from major book wholesalers, retailers, and various online outlets. For more information, please visit: www.firstdigitalmagazine.com.

Magazine Business Plan Kit

Magazine Business Plan Kit

If you're seriously thinking about publishing a magazine, then it's a good idea to start with a plan. This sample magazine business plan kit will help you map out and strategize the future of your magazine, estimate start-up and ongoing costs, outline the resources you will need, set measurable goals and objectives so you always know where you stand, evaluate and study the competition, understand your markets and how best to satisfy them, raise funds or attract investors, and most importantly, determine whether your business model can function at a profit. To find out more, please visit: www.publishyourfirstmagazine.com.

Index

A

B

C

D

E

F

G

M

N

O

P